ruben gallego

WHITE ON BLACK

Translated from the Russian by
Marian Schwartz

HARCOURT, INC.
Orlando   Austin   New York   San Diego   Toronto   London

www.HarcourtBooks.com

This is a translation of *Beloe na chernom* (St. Petersburg: Limbus Press, 2004)

Library of Congress Cataloging-in-Publication Data
Gonsales Gallego, Ruben David.
[Beloe na chernom. English]
White on black/Ruben Gallego; translated from the Russian by Marian Schwartz.
p.   cm.
I. Schwartz, Marian.   II. Title.
PG3491.96.N78B4513   2006   2005006934
ISBN-13: 978-0151-01227-5   ISBN-10: 0-15-101227-X

Text set in Adobe Garamond
Designed by Linda Lockowitz

Printed in the United States of America

First edition
K J I H G F E D C B A

Letters, just letters on the ceiling, white letters crawling slowly across a black background. They started appearing at night after one of my heart attacks. I could switch the letters around on the ceiling and string them into words and sentences. In the morning, all I had to do was store them in my computer's memory.

ON STRENGTH AND GOODNESS

People sometimes ask me whether what I write actually happened. Are the heroes of my stories real?

I answer: It did, and they are real, more than real. Naturally, my heroes are collective images from the endless kaleidoscope of my endless children's homes. What I write, though, is the truth.

The sole characteristic of my work that departs from, and at times even contradicts, the authenticity of real life is my authorial view, which may be rather sentimental, occasionally breaking into pathos. I purposely avoid writing about anything bad.

I'm convinced that life and literature have more than enough of the dark side. It's just so happened that I've witnessed too much human cruelty and hate. To describe the vileness of man's fall and bestiality is to multiply the already endless chain of interconnected blasts of evil. That's not what I want. I write about goodness, triumph, joy, and love.

I write about strength. Spiritual and physical strength. The strength each one of us has inside. The strength that breaks through all barriers to triumph. Each one of my stories is a story of triumph. Even the boy from "The Cutlet," a rather sad story, triumphs. He triumphs twice. First, when out of the chaotic mess of his useless knowledge, and for lack of a knife, he finds the only three words that have any effect on his adversary. And second, when he decides to eat the cutlets—that is, to live.

Those whose sole victory is their voluntary departure from life triumph as well. The officer who perishes in the face of a superior opponent, who dies according to regulations, is a victor. I respect such people. All the same, what's most important about this man are the stuffed toys. I'm convinced that sewing teddy bears and bunny rabbits all your life is much harder than slitting your own throat once. I'm convinced that on humanity's scales a child's delight in a new toy vastly outweighs any military victory.

This is a book about my childhood. Cruel and terrible though it was, it was still my childhood. It doesn't take much for a child to retain his love for the world, to grow up and mature: a bite of lard, a salami sandwich, a handful of figs, a blue sky, a couple of books, and a kind word. That's enough. More than enough.

The heroes of this book are strong, very strong people. All too often a person has to be strong. And good. Not everyone can let himself be good, and not everyone can overcome universal misunderstanding. All too often, goodness is taken for weakness. That's sad. It's hard to be a human being, very hard, but altogether possible. And you don't have to stand on your hind legs to do it. Not at all. I believe that.

HERO

I'm a hero. It's easy to be a hero. If you don't have hands or feet, you're either a hero or dead. If you don't have parents, rely on your hands and feet. And be a hero. If you don't have hands or feet, and in addition you've contrived to come into this world an orphan—that's it. You're doomed to be a hero to the end of your days. Or else kick the bucket. I'm a hero. I have no other choice.

I'm a little boy. It's night. It's winter. I need to go to the toilet. Calling for the attendant is pointless.

There's just one solution: crawl to the toilet.

For starters, I have to get down from the bed. There's a way to do this; I came up with it myself. I just crawl to the edge of the bed, flip onto my back, and throw my body to the floor. Wham! Ouch.

I crawl to the door, push it with my head, and crawl out of the relatively warm room into the cold, dark hallway.

At night, all the windows in the hallway are left open. It's cold, very cold. I'm naked.

It's a long way to crawl. When I crawl past the room where the attendants who look after us are sleeping I call for help. I bang my head against their door. No response. I shout. No one. Maybe I'm shouting too softly.

By the time I reach the toilet, I'm chilled to the bone.

The windows are open and there's snow on the windowsill.

I reach the toilet. I rest. I absolutely must rest before crawling back. While I'm resting, the pee in the toilet crusts over with ice.

I crawl back. I pull the blanket off the bed with my teeth, wrap myself up in it somehow, and try to fall asleep.

In the morning they dress me and take me to school. In history class I cheerfully recount the horrors of the Fascist concentration camps. I get the top mark. I always get top marks in history. I have top marks in all my subjects. I'm a hero.

THE BAYONET

A bayonet is an excellent thing. Reliable. One blow, and your opponent falls. A bayonet pierces straight through your enemy's body. A bayonet never lets you down; a bayonet kills for sure. A bullet kills at random; a bullet's a fool. A bullet might pass through on a tangent, a bullet might get stuck in the body and eat away at a human life meanly, from within. A bayonet isn't a bullet, a bayonet is cold steel, the last remnant of the nineteenth century.

There's a bayonet embossed on the cover of Nikolai Ostrovsky's first book. The blind, paralyzed writer couldn't read his own book. All he had left was running his fingers over and over the bayonet's contours. The most durable bayonet in the world is a bayonet made of paper.

The ancient Vikings were the best fighters in the world. Fearless fighters, real men, strong of spirit. A Viking who fell in battle could not be written off too soon. A Viking who fell in battle, as he departed this life, in one final burst would sink his teeth into his enemy's leg. Dying slowly, cursing your good-for-nothing life and exasperating yourself and the people close to you with endless complaints about your luckless fate is the lot of the weak. A soldier in battle doesn't care about Hamlet's timeless question. Living in battle and dying in battle are the same thing. Living at half strength and dying at half strength, living with pretense, is repugnant and vile. The greatest thing a mortal can hope for is to go down fighting. If he's lucky, if he's very lucky, he can die flying. Die clutching a horse's bridle or the controls of a fighter plane, a saber or a machine gun, a blacksmith's hammer or a chess king. If they chop your hand off in battle, it's no calamity. You can pick the blade up with your other hand. If it falls, all is not yet lost. There's still a chance, a small chance, of dying like a Viking, of clenching your enemy's heel in your teeth. Not everyone is that lucky; not everyone gets to do this. Homer and Beethoven are the happy exceptions that only confirm the remoteness of the odds. But you have to do battle, there's no other choice; any other way is dishonest and stupid.

I cried over a book. Books, like people, can be different. If you think, if you think very hard, comics are books, too. Beautiful books with beautiful pictures. Entertaining toys— paper butterflies that live for one day—comics have a huge advantage over all other books in that they don't make children cry. Books shouldn't make happy little children cry. "To be or not to be" has no meaning for them. They're children, just children, it's too early for them to be thinking. I read the book, I read it and cried. I cried out of impotence and envy. I wanted to go there, I wanted to do battle, but I couldn't. I couldn't do anything. I was used to that, but even so, I cried. There are books that change the way you look at the world, books that make you feel like dying or living differently.

If you want to understand something, you have to ask either people or books. Books are people, too. Like people, books can help; like people, books lie.

I wasn't simply reading books; I was trying to understand how the world worked. I wanted to find out how I was supposed to live in this world. I asked people, but they wouldn't tell me. I searched for the answer in books, and the books ducked the question. Books told me in detail—in great detail, even—how you were supposed to live if you had everything. Book heroes suffered, which amazed me. I, a real, living person, didn't understand them, these book people. I didn't accept their paper sufferings. They were pretending, like the teachers in school. The teachers advised me to read books, and I did. I read book after book. I read endless tedious descriptions of the pointless lives of weak and lazy people. The teachers called these people heroes, but I couldn't understand what their heroism consisted of.

D'Artagnan a hero? What kind of hero could he be if he had hands and feet? He had everything—youth, health, beauty, a saber, and the ability to fence. Where's the heroism in that? A coward and traitor who is constantly committing foolish acts for the sake of glory and riches is a hero? I read the book without understanding even half. Everyone—adults and children alike—considered the musketeers heroes. I didn't argue. Arguing was pointless. In any case, I couldn't use these heroes as my example.

I read that thick book all the way through several times. I also read the continuation of the famous tale of the brave musketeers. The continuation did not disappoint me. The unlucky freak, Monsieur Coquenard, did what a real hero is supposed to do: he died. He died, leaving his wife and his money to Porthos. Monsieur Coquenard did not arouse my sympathy, though. If that pathetic old man had had the strength and smarts to sprinkle poison into Porthos's wine,

I would have been on his side. But there are no miracles. The unfortunate cripple dragged out his miserable existence, overshadowing the deeds of the true heroes with his invalid's chair. Poor fellow.

The others were no better. Pathetic little people worthy of contempt. Insects who resembled people only in part. Bags of shit not good enough for heaven or hell. Fighters who didn't know how to live or die. Only a few of them earned my respect to any extent. Porthos, for instance. I liked Porthos much better than Coquenard. Porthos at least managed to die like a man.

Gwynplaine was a fool who suffered over nothing. Imagine, a disfigured face. Cyrano behaved a little more intelligently. If you have two strong hands and a sharp sword, beauty can be debated. And a sword is not a bad argument. Actually, Cyrano disappointed me, too. Strong in his dealings with men, he turned out to be a sniveler and a whiner in the face of love.

I envied Quasimodo. People looked on him with revulsion and pity, the way they do me. But he had hands and feet. He had all of Notre Dame de Paris.

Book heroes weren't heroes, or were heroes only in part. The very best of them behaved like men from time to time, but reluctantly, I thought. They allowed themselves to live for only a few minutes before they died. Only just before they died did I like them. Only a worthy death reconciled them to their pointless life.

Rarely did I cry over books. I had plenty of reasons to cry without some invented book grief. But one book was the real thing. This book didn't lie.

Pavka Korchagin galloped on horseback and wielded a

blade just as well as the musketeers. Pavka Korchagin was a strong, brave fellow. He fought for an idea; he didn't care about money or titles. His Red Army helmet—bearing a pitiful resemblance to a knight's—couldn't protect him from a crude bullet. His sharp blade was powerless against a Mauser. He knew this, but he went into battle. He went into the fray over and over again. Over and over again he tore into the very thick of battle. He fought and triumphed, he always triumphed. With weapon and word. When his body gave out, when his hand could no longer hold a blade, he changed weapons, and his pen became his bayonet. He managed to do that. The last knight of cold steel. The last Viking of the twentieth century.

What does a man have left when he has almost nothing? How can he justify the pathetic quasi existence of his quasi corpse? Why should he live? I didn't know then, and I don't know now. Like Pavel Korchagin, though, I don't want to die before my death. I want to live to the very end. I'm going to put up a fight. Slowly pressing the computer keys, I set down letter after letter. I'm painstakingly forging my own bayonet—my book. I know I have the right to just one blow; there's not going to be any second chance for me. I'm trying, trying hard. I know that a bayonet kills for sure. A bayonet is an excellent thing. Reliable.

DREAMS

When I was very little, I dreamed of my mama. I dreamed of her until I was six. Then I realized—or, more likely, it was explained to me—that my mama was a black-assed bitch who had abandoned me. I don't enjoy writing this, but they explained the situation to me in precisely those terms.

The people who did the explaining were big and strong and they were right about everything; therefore they were right about this minor point too. Of course, there were other grown-ups as well.

These were the teachers. The teachers told me stories about far-off lands and great writers, about how life was wonderful and every person would find himself a place on earth if only he studied well and obeyed his elders. They were always lying. Lying about everything. They told stories about the stars and continents, but they wouldn't let me go past the gate of the children's home. They talked about the equality of all people, but they took only the ambulants to the circus and the movies.

The attendants were the only ones who didn't lie. In Russian, the word for attendant, or nursemaid, is marvelous: *nyanya*. A caressing word that immediately calls to mind

Pushkin's famous line, *"Let's drink, Nyanya . . ."* Down-to-earth, hardworking women. They never lied. Once in a while they even treated us to candy. Some were mean, and some had good hearts, but they were all direct and sincere. Often you could extract the essence of something from what they said when it was impossible to get an intelligible answer from the teachers. When they gave me a piece of candy, they would say: "Poor child, better you'd died. You'd have spared yourself the suffering, and us." Or, when they were carrying out someone who had died: "Well, and thank God, his suffering's over, poor thing." Whenever I caught a cold and didn't have to go to school and was left in the sleeping wing with one of these attendants, the good-hearted woman would bring me something sweet, or some of her stewed fruit, and tell me about her children who had died at the front, about her drunk of a husband, about all kinds of interesting things. I listened and believed everything, the way children—and only children, perhaps—believe the truth. Frequently, grown-ups can't believe anything anymore. So you see, the attendants told me about the "black-assed bitch" quite simply and naturally, as if they were talking about the rain or snow.

At age six I stopped dreaming of my mama. I dreamed of becoming ambulant. Almost everyone was ambulant, even those who could barely get around on crutches. The ambulants were treated much better than we were. They were human beings. After they left the children's home they could be people society needed—bookkeepers, shoemakers, seamstresses. Many got a good education and made their way in the world. After leaving the children's home they would come to visit in expensive cars. Then we would assemble in the auditorium and be told what position this former pupil from our school now held. The stories implied that these fat, middle-aged men and women had always obeyed their elders, studied well, and earned everything by their wits and persistence. But they were ambulants! What kind of moron did I have to be to listen to their boastful talk if I knew very well what you were supposed to do after you became an ambulant? How to become an ambulant, though—that, no one ever told me.

At eight I understood one very simple idea: I'm alone and nobody needs me. Grown-ups and children alike think only of themselves. Naturally, I knew that somewhere on another planet there existed mamas and papas, grandpas and grandmas. But that was so far away and unconvincing that I relegated all those ravings to the sphere of stars and continents.

At nine I understood I was never going to walk. This was very sad. Distant lands, stars, and other joys were cut off to me. The only thing left was death. A long and useless death.

At ten I read about kamikazes. These bold fellows inflicted death on the enemy. In one nonstop flight they repaid all their debts to their homeland for the rice they'd eaten, the diapers they'd soiled, their notebooks, girls' smiles, the sun and stars, for the right to see their mama every day. This suited me. I realized no one was ever going to seat me in an airplane. I dreamed of a torpedo. A guided torpedo filled with explosives. I dreamed of stealing up to an enemy aircraft carrier very quietly and pressing the red button.

Many years have passed since then. I'm a grown man now and understand everything. Maybe that's good, but maybe that's not so good. People who understand everything are often boring and primitive. I have no right to wish for death, because my family's destiny largely depends on me. My wife and children love me, and I love them very, very much. Sometimes, though, when I lie in bed at night unable to fall asleep, I still dream of the torpedo and the red button. This naive, childish dream has never left me, and perhaps it never will.

HOLIDAY

My first memory. I'm alone and little and lying in my crib.
I'm howling. No one comes. I howl for a long time. My crib
is a regular child's bed with high barred railings. I'm lying on
my back, I hurt, and I'm wet. The walls of my crib are draped
with a solid white cover. No one's there. In front of me I see
the white ceiling; if I turn my head, I can look at the white
cover for a long time. I howl and howl. The grown-ups come
according to a schedule. When they do come, they yell at me,
feed me, and change my diaper. I love grown-ups, but they
don't love me. Let them yell, let them move me to an uncom-
fortable couch. I don't care. I just want someone to come.
Then I can see the other cribs, the table, the chairs and window. That's all. After that, they can put me back in my crib.
When they do, I howl again. They yell at me. They don't
want to pick me up, and I don't want to go into my crib. For
as long as I can remember, I was always afraid when they left
me alone. They left me alone regularly.

My first and nicest smell was a mixture of wine breath
and perfume. Sometimes women in white lab coats would
come and pick me up. Pick me up carefully, not in the usual

way. They called this a "holiday." They smelled deliciously of alcohol. They carried me off somewhere, to a big room with a table and chairs. I sat on someone's lap. The women passed me around. They gave me something delicious to eat. But nicest of all was being able to see everything. Everything around me. People's faces, the pretty plates on the tables, the bottles and glasses. Everyone was drinking wine, eating, and talking. The woman whose lap I was sitting on held me up very carefully with one hand and with the other knocked back shot after shot and nibbled on the snacks. There were different snacks, and she pinched off a tiny piece of each and put it in my mouth. No one yelled at anyone. It was warm and cozy.

A drinking party at the children's home. An ordinary drinking party, perfectly proper. The boys were drinking vodka and snacking. These were the upperclassmen. They slipped into the room quickly after lessons, sat in a corner, and appointed someone to be the lookout. They opened up jars, had a drink of vodka apiece from the same mug, and took a quick bite of something.

All of a sudden they noticed me. I was lying under a bed in the far corner of the room. My body was under the bed, my head and shoulders stuck out, and there was a book in front of me. Reading with your legs tucked under a bed is very cozy. No one bothers you.

"Ruben, crawl on over."

I set aside my book and crawl. I crawl slowly, but everyone waits patiently. I crawl up.

"How about some vodka?"

It's a rhetorical question. Everyone realizes I'm not supposed to drink vodka yet. We only started drinking vodka after we turned twelve.

Everyone laughs. They laugh kindly. Everyone's in a good mood.

"Knock it off, Seryoga, leave the kid alone. Give him something to chew on, why don't you."

Seryoga, a legless fellow, gives me a piece of bread with a slice of sausage on top. He peels a clove of garlic for me.

The boys finish their vodka and stash the empty bottle. They eat. I eat with them. We're having a good time. Everyone's having a good time. It's a holiday. If it weren't a holiday, no one would have noticed me, let alone shared food with me. I'm nobody, a rookie.

After the vodka, they drink chifir. They brew the strong black tea in a big tin and drink it slowly, taking turns. I can't drink chifir, and not just because I'm still little. Everybody knows I have a weak heart.

Seryoga takes the vodka mug, hops onto his trolley, and wheels out of the room. He comes back with an almost full mug of water. He's got the mug in one hand and is carefully pushing off the floor with the other. He puts the mug on the floor and takes a jar of jam and a spoon from the cupboard. He pours a little bit out of the common chifir jar into the mug and adds jam. A heaping spoonful of jam.

"Here," he says. "Ruben. Now you have tea with jam."

The boys are drinking chifir and I'm drinking sweet tea. It feels good. It's a holiday.

FOOD

I didn't like to eat. If I could have, I would have preferred pills like the ones in science fiction stories. I would have swallowed a pill like that and been full all day. I ate badly, and they were always coaxing me, spoon-feeding me. It was all useless.

I was lucky when I was very little. I lived in a small children's home out in the country. They fed me well and the food was delicious. The attendants were good, they always made sure all the children ate, and they worried about us.

Later there were other children's homes, other attendants, and other food. Pearl barley, wormy biscuits, rotten eggs. We had it all. But I'm going to write about something else.

I catch myself thinking that my best memories are connected with food. All the best moments of my childhood are connected with food, or rather, with the people who shared food with me, who gave me food as a token of their good will toward me. It's odd.

I don't remember where this was. I do remember people in white coats. There were a lot of us children, and we were all very little.

They brought a pineapple into the room. At the time

I thought it was very big and beautiful. They didn't cut it up right away, but let us admire it. The grown-ups themselves apparently couldn't bring themselves to destroy this beauty. Pineapples are a rarity in Russia.

The pineapple disappointed everyone. Or rather, nearly everyone. The children all tried its sharp, specific taste and refused to eat those stinging slices. Only I ate them. I remember the grown-ups' conversation.

"Let's give him more."

"What's the matter with you? What if it makes him sick?"

"Have you seen his chart? I'll bet his papa grew up on these pineapples. Maybe they have pineapples there the way we have potatoes."

They gave me more and more. The grown-ups must have found it amusing the way this odd child could eat this exotic fruit. And they couldn't bring themselves to throw out so much of value. I ate many slices of pineapple. And I didn't get sick.

They brought me to my first children's home. There were no people in white coats or rows of beds. On the other hand, there were lots of children and a television.

"What, you mean he can't sit at all? Let's put him on the couch and prop him up with pillows."

They put me on the couch, propped me up with pillows, and fed me cream of wheat with a spoon. I was so surprised that I ate the whole plate of cereal and fell asleep. The cereal was very tasty. I liked the children's home.

The hospital. Nighttime. Everyone's asleep. A nurse runs into the ward and turns on the night-light over my bed. She's wearing a fancy dress and high heels and her hair is curled and lying loose on her shoulders. She bends low over me. Her eyes are very big and happy. She smells of perfume and something else, from home, not the hospital.

"Open your mouth and close your eyes."

I obey. She puts a big piece of chocolate in my mouth. I know how you're supposed to eat chocolates. You're supposed to hold the chocolate and take little bites. Not only that, but I wanted to get a better look at this candy.

"Chew it up and swallow. Okay?"

I nod.

She turns off the night-light and runs out. I chew up the candy. My mouth fills with something sweet and stinging. I'm chewing a chocolate, and for some reason my head is spinning. I feel good. Happy.

They've moved me to another children's home. I'm crawling down the hallway and an attendant is walking toward me. It's dark in the hall, and she doesn't notice me right away. When she gets very close, she suddenly shrieks and jumps back. Then she comes closer and bends down to get a better look at me. I have swarthy skin, and my head is shaved. At first glance, in the dim light of the hallway, all you can see are my eyes, my big eyes, hanging in the air fifteen centimeters off the floor.

"A real little mover. All skin and bones. Like he just got out of Buchenwald."

It's true, I'm not very fat. At the place they brought me from, they didn't feed me very well, and I ate badly anyway.

She walks away. She comes back a couple of minutes later and puts a piece of bread and lard on the floor in front of me.

This is the first lard I've ever seen in my life, which is why I eat the lard first and then the bread. Suddenly I feel all warm and cozy, and I drift off to sleep.

It's Easter. All the attendants are dressed up. There's a holiday feel to everything—to the fact that the attendants are especially kind to us and the aides are extra watchful. I don't understand anything. You see, during holidays they show parades and marches on television. Only on New Year's is there no parade. But on New Year's there's a tree and presents.

After breakfast an attendant gives each of us a dyed egg. Inside, the egg is white, like a regular egg. I eat the whole Easter egg. It's very tasty, much tastier than the eggs they give us in the children's home. Children's-home eggs are overcooked and tough, but this one is soft and very, very tasty.

Oddly enough, no matter where I was, whether in a children's home, or a hospital, or an old folks' home, some good soul has always given me a dyed egg at Easter. And that is simply grand.

In Russia, there's a custom of honoring the dead by sharing food. On the fortieth day after someone dies, his relatives are supposed to share food—and not with just anyone they happen across, but with the most unfortunate. The more unfortunate the person fed, the more you've pleased the deceased and the greater your merit before God. But where was one to find them, the unfortunates, in the most fortunate country in the world? And so they came to the gate of our children's home, poor devils, with their bags, baskets, and packages. They brought candies, cookies, and buns. They brought pirozhki and blini—whatever they could. Our indefatigable aides—young teachers waiting for a proper position to open up in the classroom—tried to drive them away, most often without success.

Our attendants, taking advantage of their official position, would bring the "funeral food" through the gate of the children's home, despite a strict prohibition against this.

Luckiest of all were the attendants who worked with us, the nonambulants. We were fed separately, and the aides were far away. One attendant cleverly slipped a pot of fruit jelly through the front door. Not only that, but since we were the most unfortunate of all, the candies fed to us were much more expensive.

For our part, we knew that you weren't supposed to say thank you for the funeral food and that when they gave you these treats, you weren't supposed to smile.

I was lying in the garden. "The garden" was what we called the few apple trees that grew next to the home. It took me a long time to crawl to the garden, so I was tired and lying on my back, resting. All the ambulants were far away, watching a movie at the club maybe. They'd been taken somewhere—I don't remember where. I was lying there waiting for an apple to fall not too far away. But I had much better luck than that.

A withered old woman was clambering over the fence. The fence was two meters high, but that didn't stop the granny. She hopped down, looked both ways, and walked toward me. After soberly examining my hands and feet, she asked tentatively: "An orphan, maybe?" I nodded. Such luck she had never anticipated: crooked hands and feet and an orphan to boot. She put her basket on the ground, threw back the towel covering the contents, took out a blin, gave it to me, and commanded, "Eat." I quickly began eating blini while she hurried me along, repeating: "Auntie Varvara, pray for Auntie Varvara." But all good things end quickly. An aide was already walking around the corner.

"Why are outsiders on our grounds? Who let her in? What are you doing here?"

And then to me:

"What are you doing?"

What was I doing? I was chewing my third blin. I was chewing fast, because I still had half a blin in my hand and I wanted to finish all of it.

The nimble old woman had already snatched up her basket and hurdled the fence. I quickly finished the blin. The aide stood there a while, smiled at something, and went away.

These were the first blini I'd eaten in my life.

They're moving me again, from one home to another. The fun begins at the train station, where they give me ice cream and lemon soda. The ice-cream bar is big and coated with chocolate. As soon as the train starts moving, the attendant and nurse go off "for a stroll," as they put it. "Hey, go for a stroll?" They come back with two Georgians. One Georgian is old and gray, the other's a little younger. They're all drinking vodka and having a good time. They cut me a big hunk of sausage; they give me hard-boiled eggs and lemon soda. The gray-haired Georgian keeps cutting sausage, making sandwiches, and telling me: "Eat, you eat, children should eat well." There's an awful lot of food, and no one's keeping track of it. It's getting dark and I can look out the window all I want and eat sausage. I feel like riding and riding and looking out the window. I think about how if all the grown-ups on earth were given a lot of vodka and sausage, they would be kind and all the children would be happy.

I'm in my last children's home, the best children's home in the world. In front of me is my breakfast: a little mashed potatoes, a nice tomato half, a buttered roll, and tea. I know for certain that today isn't a holiday, so then why did they give me potatoes? I try the tea: it's sweet. A fresh tomato is a delicacy in itself. I eat it all and realize that I have had fantastic luck. I've landed in paradise.

Katya and I are living in a half-basement because her parents won't recognize our marriage. The apartment belongs to my teacher, one of the finest women on earth. She moved us into her apartment and went to live at her dacha.

On her way home from the university Katya buys pelmeni. She cooks the whole package at once. I know what pelmeni are—little noodle balls filled with meat. They used to give them to us at the children's home, four per kid.

"How many are we each going to eat?" I ask Katya.

She gives me a strange look.

"What, you mean you counted them?"

Katya serves us pelmeni. She eats a plate of them, but I can't get down more than six. I realize that in this strange, unregimented world, people don't count the pelmeni.

"Don't throw out the pelmeni water," I advise Katya practically. "You can make soup from it."

A few days later we're visiting her parents and Katya is eating pelmeni again. Her mama takes the pot off the table and is about to go to the kitchen.

"Mama, don't pour out the water. You can make soup from it," Katya says automatically.

The next day, when Katya leaves for classes at the university, her mama tiptoes up to our building and leaves a fresh chicken by the door. The ice has been broken.

When Katya leaves for work, I'm left one on one with the most enchanting of women. We're living in an apartment with her grandmother.

She stops by my room and sits down facing me:

"Well, so when are you gonna croak?"

"Hold your horses," I reply. "When it's time, that's when I'll croak. You're no spring chicken yourself. Or are you planning on living forever?"

"What makes you so useful, no hands, no feet? You can't hammer a nail."

"Do you have a marking pen?"

"Yes."

"You go all through the apartment, and everywhere you need a nail, put a mark. Believe me, the nails'll get hammered in."

And so we pass the time in heart-to-heart conversation. Grandma tells me about her youth and her relatives. Her stories lead me to believe that her entire clan is nothing but scoundrels and rogues.

After a while she goes to the kitchen and rattles the pots. She comes in.

"Ruben. I made borscht. Are you going to eat it or are you afraid I'll poison you?"

"Let's have the borscht. I'm not afraid of being poisoned. I've eaten worse."

She brings me the borscht. The borscht is delicious. At the bottom of the plate is a big piece of duck meat.

When Alla was pregnant, we were living hand to mouth. Alla ate bread with used grease. I couldn't eat grease; I ate bread and sunflower oil. (In the children's homes, bread drizzled with sunflower oil and sprinkled with salt was considered a treat.) That year, for the first time, I had trouble with my digestion. We were also making pea soup. Alla didn't eat soup, and I ate nothing else. It was a hundred times easier for me than for her; I could eat soup and I wasn't pregnant. When Maya was born, Alla decided to breast-feed her. Natural nourishment is very healthy. But Maya wasn't feeding well, and Alla's milk was greenish. And so was Maya's poop. All this time, Alla was eating nothing but potatoes. Alla's a healthy person, and she needs a lot more food than I do. What she eats at one meal I eat in a day. We decided that switching Maya to formula would be cheaper than providing Alla with proper nourishment.

A friend came over.
    "How are you doing?"
    "Fine."
    "What are you eating?"
    "Pea soup."
    "With potatoes?"
    "Naturally."
    "We've been eating pea soup without potatoes for more than a week."
    I've been eating pea soup for just three days. I have a sack of potatoes.

Maya is one and a half. She's refused to eat her hot cereal. I take it and calmly finish it. Maya asked for some sausage first, then gingerbread. We don't have either one, but that's not the point. If you're hungry, you'll eat anything; if not, then run along (a children's-home rule). Maya walks around the apartment and thinks. Then she calmly goes over to Alla and says, "Mama, cook potatoes." We eat potatoes with salt and sunflower oil, and I remember how in the children's home we cooked potatoes after lights out with the help of a jury-rigged immersion heater. What I didn't get until I was fifteen (only upperclassmen could cook potatoes), Maya already had from birth.

Alla brings Maya home from nursery school. Alla is laughing. She ran into the cook, who proudly told her that today at kindergarten there was a chicken for the midday meal. "So big and fat, everyone got a piece." There are more than a hundred children at the nursery school. And there was one chicken, or rather, one and a half. I laugh, too.

I'm glad that Maya is going to nursery school. She has lots of friends there, and they sculpt with play dough and paint pictures. Not only that, but when she comes home from nursery school, Maya eats everything she's given and doesn't fuss.

On the way home from nursery school, Maya asks Alla to buy her some rusks.

"What's the matter with you? We have money now. If you want, I'll buy you a pastry or something else."

"No, rusks."

Alla buys the rusks. Maya sits down at the table and gnaws away at her rusks all evening. It turns out, at snack time the teachers had given the children a rusk apiece, and Maya wanted more. At the children's home they gave us two rusks apiece.

When I was living at the old folks' home, one thing amazed me. In the dining room, after the midday meal, they would pass out bones. Ordinary beef bones from the soup. Only war veterans were supposed to get bones. The meat had been carefully cut off the bones, but if you were clever, you could still get more. The veterans crowded in front of the pass-through, cursed, and reeled off their accomplishments and ranks. Recently I asked my friend from the home whether they still gave out bones there.

"What's the matter with you? They haven't cooked anything with bones for a long time. There are no bones."

THE ATTENDANTS

There were very few of them. Genuine *nyanyas*—caring attendants, full of kindness and concern. I don't remember their names, or rather, I don't remember all the names of all the good-hearted ones. Among ourselves we divided them up into "evil" and "good." In that children's-home world, the line between good and evil seemed obvious. For a long time I've tried—unsuccessfully—to shake the bad children's-home habit of dividing all people into us and them, smart and stupid, good and evil. What can I do? I grew up where there was a fine line between life and death and meanness and nastiness were standard. So were sincerity and goodness. It was all a jumble. The constant need to choose between bad and good must have fostered this categorical streak in me.

The good attendants believed in God. All of them. There, I've gone and divided people up into categories again. I can't seem to get away from it.

Believing in God was forbidden. They told us there was no God. Atheism was the norm. Nowadays hardly anyone would credit this, but that's how it was. I don't know whether any of the teachers were believers. They probably were. The teachers were forbidden to talk to us about that. Making the sign of the cross or dying an Easter egg could get a teacher fired—but not an attendant. An attendant's wages were low and there was a lot of work. There weren't many people eager to wash floors and change children's pants. The bosses simply turned a blind eye to the believing attendants. And they did believe. They believed no matter what. They prayed for a long time when they were on night duty, lighting a candle they'd brought along. They made the sign of the cross over us at night. At Easter they brought us dyed eggs and blini. It was forbidden to bring food into the children's home, but what could the strict bosses do to these illiterate women?

There were just a few good attendants. I remember them all. Right now I'll try to tell a story about one of them. This is a real story, told to me by an attendant. I'll try to retell what my childish memory retained, as accurately as I can.

"I've been working here a long time. When I arrived, I looked and there were little children, some without feet, some without hands. And every one was dirty. You wash one, then he crawls across the floor—and he's dirty again. Some you have to spoon-feed, some you have to wash every hour. I was so tired. My first night shift I didn't get a wink of sleep. They'd brought in a new one, and he kept calling for his mama all night long. I sat by his bed, took his hand, and stayed like that with him until morning. I cried and cried. In the morning I went to the priest to ask for his blessing to quit. 'I can't do it,' I said, 'I can't watch this. I feel so sorry for everyone, it breaks my heart.' But the priest wouldn't give his blessing. He said, 'This is your cross to the end of your days.' I begged and pleaded with him. But then I worked for a while and learned to live with it. Still it's hard. I write down the names of all the children I take care of on a piece of paper. I have a notebook at home, and that's where I write all of you down. And at Easter I light a candle for each one of you. It's getting to be a lot of candles. It's expensive. But still I light one and say an Our Father for each of you. Because the Lord told us to pray for all the innocent children. But you have such a strange name, Ruben. Must be Armenian. The Armenians are Christians, I know that for sure. Not Armenian, you say? Then I thought, since his parents don't come to visit, they must be Basurmans or something. A christened soul wouldn't abandon her child. They're bitches—forgive me, Lord, old fool that I am, no matter how hard you try, you still sin. But you're going to be in my notebook without a last name recorded. Your last name is so queer, I wouldn't be able to write it. Everyone's written down with a last name, except you. In prayer you're only supposed to say the first name, but it's still not good that there's no last name."

What can I add to this story? I grew up, read scads of different books, and now think I'm very smart. Thank you to my teachers, who taught me how to read. Thank you to the Soviet state, which raised me. Thank you to the smart Americans, who created the computer and gave me the chance to type this text with my left index finger.

Thank you to all the good-hearted attendants for teaching me about goodness, for the warmth in my heart that I carried through all my trials. Thank you for what can't be expressed in words, or entered on a computer, or measured. Thank you for your love and Christian mercy, for the fact that I'm a Catholic, and for my little children. For everything.

THE LADS

There were ten of us on the ward. Or rather, nine. We didn't count Vovochka. Vovochka couldn't talk. He couldn't do anything, just eat and shit. Often he woke us up with his yelling. As always, he was hungry. He could eat a lot, however much they gave him. They gave him the same as everyone else, but that wasn't enough for him, so he would yell. A twelve-year-old baby.

There was also me, and Vasilek. Vasilek looked twenty. He had paralyzed legs. He was as healthy as an ox. Or rather, as lots of mentally retarded people. Once he grabbed the leg of an attendant who was teasing him and she couldn't get away. The bruise on her leg took a very long time to heal. The attendants teased him, the harmless bull, and gave him a smack on the back as they walked by or said something dirty, and then he would jack off noisily all night long, giving grounds for new jokes. Actually, they treated him well and always served him a double portion.

I'm a nine-year-old boy. Imagine a paralyzed little person. He's lying on the floor, his head propped up on his elbows, and rocking from side to side. He's doing something, but you can't quite tell what. He's crawling. I crawled fast. In half an hour I could crawl three hundred meters if I wasn't tired. Though every ten or fifteen meters I had to rest. But I could crawl! Vasilek and I were the only ones in the ward who could crawl. That's what distinguished us from the rest.

There were seven of them. I don't remember all their names. Not that I was supposed to know their names. Only Sashka Poddubny could sit up, so in the mornings the attendants would seat him on the floor in front of a low table. The rest lay in their beds around the clock. They were called "the lads." The respect for them at the children's home was absolute; even the head honcho would come to consult with them. We were the only ones with a television in our room, and we could watch it whenever we wanted.

I ended up in that ward by chance. When they brought me, one of the lads had just died. This was unlucky cot No. 3. Three boys had slept in it before me, and they had all died. No one wanted to take it, but I was the new kid. Then they wanted to move me to another ward, but Sashka Poddubny asked them to keep me there. That's another story.

One day Sashka needed to go to the toilet, but Vasilek wasn't in the room.

I had a choice: crawl after an attendant or try to help him myself. I took the elastic of his trousers in my teeth, pulled them off, pushed the bedpan over, and he pissed. Now, according to the unspoken rule of the children's home, I could ask him a favor, too. I summoned all my nerve and asked him to let me read one of his books. He had a lot of books. He was constantly reading something or translating from German.

"Take *The Three Musketeers*."

"I've already read *The Three Musketeers,* and it's a children's book. Give me *Solaris.*"

"You won't understand anything in it."

"Yes, I will."

"You're stubborn; that's good. Take *Solaris* and then tell me what you understood."

I read *Solaris* in one Sunday. When Sashka asked me what I'd understood from the book, I replied, "It was stupid for the hero to fly off, because he should have cleared things up with the woman, on Earth, first." Sashka said that I was still little and didn't understand anything. But after that he started lending me books. All in all, I was lucky. The lads treated me well.

Our volunteers came to see us. Our volunteers were students from the teachers' college.

They assembled us in the auditorium and our volunteers sang little songs for us and left. Or rather, not everyone left. According to the volunteer schedule, students had to do certain activities with us, help us with our lessons, and so on. But most of them looked at us as if we were lepers. I read that expression, "as if they were lepers," later, and I liked it a lot. How else can I convey their bugged-out eyes and poorly concealed disgust?

Some did come, though. Strangely, it was the female students who weren't exactly setting the world on fire. Innate goodness and compassion, maybe curiosity, too, brought them to see us over and over again.

One of these girls stopped in to visit.

"Boys, can I help you with anything?"

"Want some chifir?"

"What?"

"Strong tea."

"Sure."

"Then get me the kettle out from under the mattress and the can from the night table, go get some water, and set it all up under the bed."

This was Moscow Vovka talking. That was his nickname: Moscow. Why, I don't know.

This student visited us several times, and the lads treated her to chocolates and badgered her with jokes. It was nice and fun to be around her.

One day she had stayed longer than usual and it was time for her to go. No one wanted to let her, naturally.

"Boys, I have to do my physics and math, and it's not something I can just dash off."

"What year are you in?"

"My second."

"Do you have your textbook with you?"

"In my bag."

"Get it out and read a problem."

This was Genka, talking from the corner cot.

She did, and sat down to read.

"But I don't understand any of it."

"Me, neither. I'm just in first year. Read it out loud."

"The formulas too?"

"The formulas too."

She read her textbook and we rejoiced that she still hadn't left. We had no doubt that Genka would solve all her problems.

She read for a long time, and then Genka told her to sit down at the table and write.

"But you can't see what I'm writing."

"Can you, though?"

"Yes."

"Well then, write."

He dictated the solutions to all of her problems, then fell silent.

"Can I check the answers? I have the answers written out here."

"Go ahead."

"It all matches! How did you do that? Without looking at my notebook. You're so little!"

Genka weighed ten kilos. Not only could he not walk, but there was also something wrong with his thyroid and he didn't grow. Usually they pulled a blanket up to his chin and the face of an eight-year-old boy looked out. Actually that was for the best. Occasionally they carried him outside. Vasilek and I could crawl onto the pavement by ourselves, but the others didn't get to see the outside.

"I'm eighteen. I'm as 'little' as you."

"Oh, boys"—she called them boys, which no one else did anymore. "And I thought you were still in elementary school."

"Officially we're in second year. But some of us have stayed in the same class for two years. That's just because we have a children's-home director with a good heart. He doesn't want to cart us off to the old folks' home. There'd be no one to take care of us there, and we'd die."

"But why don't you enroll at the institute? You'd be top students."

"They only accept ambulants at the institute."

She gathered her things very quickly and left. I crawled

out into the hallway. It was raining, and I wanted to crawl to the main door.

It was chilly—late autumn or early spring. They never shut the main door and I liked to crawl right up to the entrance and watch the rain. Occasional drops of rain would fall inside, fall on me. It felt good, and sad.

That time, though, my place by the door was taken. Leaning heavily against the doorjamb stood that same student, smoking greedily, taking deep drags. And crying. I don't remember what she was wearing. All I remember is her high-heeled shoes. She was very pretty. I thought I would never see such a pretty girl again. She was smoking and crying. Then she finished her cigarette and went out into the rain. Without a raincoat or umbrella.

She stopped coming to see us.

A commission arrived from Moscow. The director was slapped with a punishment, and all the lads were taken away to an old folks' home. The lads' aide came to see us in our classroom. "Now I'm going to work with you until you graduate." I had gone into my fifth year, elementary school was over, and now we were supposed to have "our" classroom director and "our" aide.

A month after the lads were taken to the old folks' home, she went to visit her former charges. She came back and told us everything.

Of the eight of them, only Genka had survived. The old folks' home was made up of separate barracks-type buildings. The elderly and the handicapped were distributed according to their degree of disability. Our lads lay in a separate barracks, with the goners. Urine dripped from their beds, which were stretched out in rows along the walls. No one came near them. The aide had brought them big cans of fruit salad. Here's what she said about Genka: "He's a nasty one. 'Take the fruit salad away,' he says. 'The ambulants are going to eat it all up anyway.'"

I asked her what was going to happen to me when I grew up. Would they take me away to an old folks' home, too, and would I die?

"Naturally."

"But I'll be fifteen; I don't want to die so soon. Does that mean it's all for nothing? Why should I study, then?"

"Nothing is for nothing. You have to study because you're being fed for free. And anyway, have you learned your lessons?"

After that, I underwent a dramatic change. Tears would well up at the drop of a hat and I'd cry. Cajoling didn't help, and neither did threats. I would shout at the top of my lungs.

They called in the doctor. A young fellow arrived, sat down in front of me on the floor, smiled, and asked me something. I smiled back. I didn't want to talk to him, but in the end, I had to.

"Why do you cry so often?"

"I don't."

"Why did you cry yesterday?"

"I was crawling around, I banged my head, and I started crying."

"I don't believe you. Your teacher told me everything. You cry all the time. That's not normal. Why don't you want to talk to me?"

"Because you're a psychiatrist. They're all so nice in the beginning, but then they take you away to the hospital. And in the hospital they give you shots, and give you pills to make you like Vasilek."

"Who told you that nonsense? No one's going to take you away. And who's this Vasilek?"

"Moscow Vovka told me about the hospital."

"And where's your Vovka now?"

"Dead. They're all dead. They were good, and smart. And Sashka Poddubny lent me his nice books to read. Now they're gone, but Vasilek's alive. They took him to a different home, a good one, because he can crawl and go to the toilet himself."

"Who told you they all died?"

"The aide. She also told me they're going to take me away too, when I'm fifteen. I'm ten now."

The smiling aide looked at the doctor perplexedly and said: "Well, and what of it? What's going on? I told the whole class that." The doctor lit a cigarette. That was the first time I'd ever seen a grown man smoke right in the ward. For some reason, I liked him.

"Are you afraid of me?"

"Yes."

He wasn't mean at all. He finished his cigarette, looked at me, and left.

Genka died very soon after.

AMERICA

We were supposed to hate that country. That was the custom. We were supposed to hate all the capitalist countries, but especially America. Our enemies—the bourgeoisie, who drank the blood of the working class—lived in America. American imperialism was making an atom bomb with our name on it. The workers in America were constantly starving and dying, and an endless stream of people hoping to change their citizenship kept pouring into the Soviet embassy in the United States. That's what they taught us, and we believed it.

I loved America. I'd loved it since I was nine. I was nine when they told me there were no handicapped people in America. They were killed. All of them. If a handicapped child was born into a family, the doctor gave the child a fatal injection.

"Now do you understand, children, how lucky we were to be born in our country? In the Soviet Union, we don't kill our handicapped children. We teach you, treat you, and feed you for free. You have to study well so you can acquire a useful profession."

I don't want them to feed me for free, and I can never have a useful profession. I want the injection, the fatal injection. I want to go to America.

RETARD

I'm a retard. That's not an insult, just a statement of fact. The medical books say that if I can't walk, then I'm too retarded for an independent existence, for basic survival. Ever since I was a child I've known that there are two ways to be retarded: mildly and severely. Someone mildly retarded is intellectually backward but can live in society without outside assistance. As the standard example of someone mildly retarded they usually cite a person who through the efforts of teachers and health workers learns to be a house painter or janitor. Teachers taught me to solve complex equations, and health workers dosed me assiduously with medicines and solicitously applied hard plaster casts—but their efforts were futile. I'm still not strong enough to lift a paintbrush.

One of my first childhood memories is of a conversation I overheard between some grown-ups.

"You say he's smart. But he can't walk!"

Nothing's changed since then. My whole life people have talked about my disability in terms of the possibility or impossibility of my performing mechanical actions: walking,

eating, drinking, using the toilet. But the main thing never changed: I couldn't walk. Hardly anything else ever interested the grown-ups. You can't walk, so you're a retard.

Another children's home, another move. I was moved to this home from the clinic where they'd been trying to get me on my feet for two years—without success. The treatment was simple. They would put my twisted legs in casts and then periodically cut the plaster in certain places, press on the joints, and set my legs in a new position. After a year and a half my legs were straight. They tried to put me on crutches but realized that was pointless and discharged me. During the treatment my legs hurt all the time and I couldn't think straight. According to law, every schoolchild in the Soviet Union had the right to an education. Those who could went to the classrooms at the clinic; the teacher went to the wards to see the others. A teacher came to see me a couple of times too, but when she became convinced of my impenetrable obtuseness, she left me in peace. The teachers pitied the poor child and gave me a "satisfactory" in all my subjects. Thus was I promoted from grade to grade.

When they put me in the clinic, I was in my second year; when they discharged me I went into my fourth. All as it should be, all according to law. They carried me into the classroom and set me on the floor.

A math lesson was in progress. I was in luck. That day the class had been given a test. A math test is a big deal, and for this serious undertaking the school's pedagogical council had scheduled a double period, two classes, each forty-five minutes long.

The teacher asked me a couple of questions, ascertained

that the boy needed to be put in the second-year class, and settled down. She summoned an attendant and told her to take me back to the sleeping wing.

The attendant arrived. She took a look at me.

"I just carried him in, and now I have to carry him out? I'm not your mule. I have rights, too. And they call themselves educated. And now, just because they didn't figure it out ahead of time, I have to strain myself? If it wasn't for the war, I might have been a teacher, too."

The attendant's voice got louder and louder. The teacher listened carefully and finally resigned herself. She politely asked the attendant to leave and apologized for disturbing her. The attendant left and the test could begin.

The teacher quickly wrote the problems on the board. When she finished, she sat down.

I looked at the board but didn't understand anything. Instead of numbers, the problems had letters. I knew perfectly well what plus and minus were—before I'd come to the clinic I'd been the best student of all—but the multiplication signs looked like simple errors.

"There's a mistake in the examples," I blurted out. "Why did you write letters instead of numbers? You can't add letters."

"That's not a mistake. Those letters do in fact stand for numbers. Which numbers the letters stand for is exactly what we need to find out. That is called solving an equation."

"You mean, if one plus x equals three, then x equals two? That's like a brainteaser in a magazine."

"That's right, more or less."

"Then why is x written between two numbers in the second example?"

"That's not the letter x. It's the multiplication sign. You can write it either as a dot or as the letter *x*. I wrote an *x* on the board so that the people in the back rows could see it better."

I didn't know what multiplication was. For some reason the doctors in the hospital were more worried about how much two times two is, and three times three, than anything in the world. If I gave a wrong answer, they laughed loudly and told me the right one, and sometimes gave me a piece of candy or a cookie. If they'd explained right away that multiplication is consecutive addition, that wouldn't have made things any easier for me. My legs hurt so badly, and I didn't like the doctors.

The teacher explained multiplication to me.

"Why am I explaining all this to you?" the teacher continued. "You don't even know your multiplication tables."

"Yes, I do, but only to five. I also remember that six times six is thirty-six."

"And seven times eight?"

"Just a sec."

I started adding the numbers out loud. I gave her the correct answer.

"Smart boy!" the teacher praised me.

"It's easy," I said. "When you explain it, everything's easy. Tell me some more."

"You wouldn't understand."

"Yes, I would. You just said yourself I was a smart boy."

The teacher walked briskly to the board and wrote the lesson. She wrote and wrote. From time to time she stopped and asked me, "Understand?" I understood everything. She told me about mathematics, and I kept interrupting her with questions. Go on, I begged, go on. We were smiling at each other. It was all so easy.

"That's it. That's everything. I've told you everything you should know as of today as a fourth-year student."

"Can I take the test?"

"I'm not sure you'll pass, but you can give it a try."

I tried.

The hour and a half passed very quickly, and the class handed in their tests. The teacher leaned down, took the sheet of paper from me, and looked it over quickly. Then she looked at me. Her eyes were cold and alien—not like just before, at the board. I'd understood everything.

It's not all that hard to be a retard. Everyone looks right past you, they ignore you. You're not a person, you're nothing. But sometimes, out of innate goodness or professional necessity, the person I'm talking to figures out that inside, I'm just like everyone else. At that moment, indifference is replaced by delight, then the delight by dull despair in the face of reality.

I didn't look at the teacher. They were all the same. I was sure that at this moment she was thinking about what everyone in her place thinks about: my legs. My legs were the main thing. Mathematics was a silly distraction.

SASHA

We'd known each other since we were five. He used to insult
me. Then we became friends. His mama often treated me to
candies, and once she gave me a windup toy. A command-
ing, strong, and very good woman, she had raised a fine son.
Only recently—about five years ago—I learned that she'd
wanted to adopt me. They wouldn't let her. When I, a grown
man by then, asked her why she had wanted me, she understood perfectly and answered simply:

"Sasha wouldn't have been so bored. You could have
played together. You could have gone to the institute, because
you're smart, not like my dunce. I would have made a professor out of you."

I looked into the eyes of this smart Russian woman and
believed that if they'd let her, she'd have knocked down every
wall, gone through every trial, carried me in her arms to lectures, but she would have made a professor of mathematics
out of this black-eyed Spanish boy. Neither a doctor nor a
teacher, she discerned in the eyes of a five-year-old boy what
so many medical commissions would attempt and fail to find.
I know she wouldn't have bothered to read the diagnoses of

my "retarded brain activity" or "mental debility." She had
seen my eyes.

I'm going to write about her son Sasha, though. A boy
who had a mama.

I can barely remember that distant childhood when we were
tots. I only really got to know Sasha when fate brought us together in another one of my children's homes.

He would crawl down the hall singing:

> *Into the ring the strongman came,*
> *A single shrug and he snapped the chain.*

Sasha was very different from us. His mama, a big boss
in commerce, had raised him simply. She had taken him to
work with her and shown him the practical side of life. He
knew about accounts and bills, how goods in short supply
got distributed, and why they gave us so little hot cereal at
breakfast.

He would crawl down the hall singing. He had a loud
voice that could be heard far away. He greeted the attendants
and teachers he met loudly. He called them "staff."

He'd been sent to school late. This was why he was much
older than his classmates. His mama had put a lot of time
and effort into trying to cure him. Like all mamas, she
wanted to see her son healthy and happy.

I was stunned by his loud singing. I didn't like the way
he talked to the attendants. Too often he used the familiar
"you" with them. "Hey, Manya, I'm not doing so hot, give
me a little more cereal. And some for this guy, too. You think
just because he doesn't have parents or anyone to stand up
for him you don't have to feed him?" At the time, I didn't

realize that he was using this intentional rudeness to conceal his shyness. I considered attendants demigods, but when it came to crudeness and swearing, Sasha could give as good as he got.

At the time, I didn't understand anything.

Sasha was sent a package. Sasha's mama realized that life in a children's home wasn't all milk and honey, so she sent him huge care packages. Loving mother that she was, she wanted Sasha to have friends and to study in school, which was why she'd brought him to the children's home in the first place. She took him home for all school vacations and for the summer, and she made his life at the children's home as pleasant as she could by sending packages and leaving him money.

Mamas varied. The very foolish mamas brought and sent their children candy. The smart mamas brought them lard, garlic, and home canning—regular food.

Sasha's mama wasn't just a smart mama; she was also a big boss. She would send fancy packages with chocolate and canned meat, canned pineapple, and avocado juice.

That day he received two packages at once, each weighing eleven kilos. Sasha was particularly proud of that weight.

"According to Soviet postal regulations, private individuals are allowed packages weighing ten kilos, but"—and here he paused—"in exceptional cases they accept packages up to eleven kilos."

We didn't understand anything about postal regulations then, but we shared Sasha's joy in full. The bigger the packages, the better. That was obvious.

An aide brought him the two packages, grunting and cursing all doting parents.

"Sasha, according to children's-home rules I can't give you more than two hundred grams of food at one time. Your ration is balanced, and it's bad for you to overeat. I have to check its quality in advance."

She shouldn't have said that.

"And are you going to check this with a special instrument or, excuse me, by tasting? I don't see any instrument. So let's make a deal. You check a can of meat and a can of pineapple, leave me the rest, and we'll go our separate ways. Okay?"

"How could you think such a thing? I don't need your meat. Take what you like and I'll put your packages away."

"Then let's do this. I'm not going to choose anything right now, and you put the packages away. Tomorrow you can bring them back, and I won't take anything again. You're required to bring me these packages. And you'll bring them to me every day—for a couple of months, until my mama comes. And then you'll explain to my mama about overeating and food quality. Believe me, she's in the trade and she knows everything about food quality."

The aide wasn't exactly thrilled by the prospect of a chat with Sasha's mother.

Sasha was a clever boy. He understood that you have to leave your opponent an out.

"Here's an idea! For now, you just check all the expiration dates on the cans and boxes and take out the ones that have expired. And don't worry about the two hundred grams. I'm not going to eat the food alone or in one night."

The aide was pleased at this turn of events. No one wanted to quarrel with Sasha's mother. Not only that, but she realized his mother wasn't going to send her son just anything. She conscientiously checked all the foods—so there wouldn't be any that had expired. Sasha could keep his packages, and he, with a lordly gesture, offered the aide a can of meat. The aide refused. Then Sasha took a can of pineapple out of the box.

"You have children. Please give this to them."

The aide hesitated. She would have liked to bring her children the pineapple, but she was still angry at Sasha, at his way of talking to her, a representative of authority and an adult. "For the children, the children," Sasha repeated and looked her in the eye. Suddenly the aide smiled, took the pineapple, and left. She was a good woman and realized that Sasha wasn't ridiculing her.

The Soviet Union was a country of universal shortages. Shortages are when something isn't for sale and can't be bought for any price. The workers at the children's home often came to Sasha asking him to "obtain" something they couldn't. Usually Sasha refused. He didn't want to play these grown-up games. He wasn't mean or greedy, he just knew that his mama was in no position to supply everyone with the things they couldn't get. The aide asked him to "obtain" buckwheat groats. There was a shortage of groats. Her mama, a diabetic, needed groats. Her mama didn't eat anything, or rather, she needed a strict diet. Buckwheat groats was one of the foods she was allowed. Sasha wrote his mama a letter, and she sent the groats.

The aide brought Sasha the package. In it were two kilos of groats. She looked at Sasha. And waited.

"Buckwheat groats, top quality," said Sasha, "price, forty-eight kopeks a kilo. Here are two kilos. That will be ninety-six kopeks."

"Fine, Sasha. I'll write down that you have ninety-six kopeks."

The problem was that children at the home were forbidden to have cash.

Foolish mamas and papas would give the money to the aide. The child could ask the aide for something, and the next day the person on duty would bring his order. This was how you could buy candies or a pencil, for example. But an aide could not be asked to buy anything forbidden. Not only wine and cigarettes, but canned fish, eggs, pastries, and all homemade foods were forbidden. I don't have to explain why we prized cash much more highly.

"No. That won't work. This isn't business. You already have my fifty rubles there. You won't give me the ninety-six kopeks?"

"No. It's forbidden. And what are you going to do with raw groats anyway?"

"I'll sell them to Dusya. She's an attendant and she couldn't care less about what you forbid."

"But I need the groats for my mama. You promised."

"I don't have anything against your mama. Let her eat buckwheat groats with pleasure. But I promised to sell you the groats, not give them."

"Fine. Take a ruble and we're quits."

"No. You owe me exactly ninety-six kopeks. I don't have four kopeks."

The aide decided to play along. She went for change.

The deal went through.

For breakfast they've given us buckwheat groats. Buckwheat groats are a rarity at the children's home. They've given us two spoonfuls of groats apiece and we're happy. Only Sasha isn't. He's spewing obscenities, and the veins on his neck are bulging. He slings a curt "Swine," takes his portion of groats from the table, and crawls to the room where the attendants are eating.

Sasha has the torso of a healthy person. His legs are twisted into an unimaginable pretzel, and one arm is paralyzed. He crawls toward the attendants' room, opens the door with his head, and with his healthy arm hurls the plate of groats into the room.

Sitting at the table in the attendants' room is an attendant with her daughter and husband. In front of each is a full plate of groats.

The man lifts his head from his plate. He sees Sasha and hears what he's saying. Sasha is ranting about how the attendant is not only getting fat on someone else's misery but is also feeding her fat-faced daughter and her fancy man. Naturally, Sasha doesn't use exactly these words. He expresses himself in normal Russian, spiced with some choice curses. I won't try to repeat what he says. The man drops his spoon of groats and all he says is: "Manya, let's get out of here." Sasha crawls away from the door and they go out.

Manya returns with a shiner under her eye and a full pot of groats. There'd been plenty in the dining room, and she'd just been too lazy to carry out the full pot.

Sasha was accused of smoking. He always had money, so he could even have bought expensive cigarettes. But he didn't smoke. On principle.

That day, he stocked up on cigarettes, crawled to the door of the teachers' room, and lit up. He smoked intently, inhaling deeply. The teachers walked up and looked at the impudent boy but didn't do anything about it. Cigarette smoke filled the hallway and was already filtering into the teachers' room. Finally, the school's director came.

We had a good director.

He squatted in front of Sasha.

"Put out the cigarette."

Sasha did.

"Finally! I thought I was going to have to smoke them all."

"What are you smoking?"

"Kosmos. Filthy stuff, of course, but at least there's a filter."

"Why were you smoking outside the teachers' room?"

"I was waiting for you."

"What for? You know smoking is bad for your health. Even filtered cigarettes."

"I don't smoke. You think I'm fool enough to poison myself and pay money to do it on top of that? It's just that they accused me of smoking. I don't care, but the aide is sure I'm sneaking around. If I decide to smoke, I'll smoke out in the open. My health is my own business. But I won't let anyone suspect me of sneaking around. If she wants me to smoke so badly, I'll smoke right in front of her."

"You mean, you were insulted by her lack of trust so you decided to protest right here?"

"Yes."

"Fine. I'll have a talk with her. Do you have any cigarettes left?"

"Two and a half packs."

"Will you give them to me?"

"These are pretty expensive cigarettes."

The director smiled and fumbled in his pocket for money. He took the cigarettes away, gave Sasha the money, and walked into the teachers' room.

That children's home had a very good director.

We had fine teachers working with us. People inspired by their profession. Of course, the teachers had it much easier than the attendants. They didn't have to take care of us. For me, a teacher's opinion meant nothing compared with an attendant's. Nevertheless, the teachers were useful members of society, whereas I was a useless hunk of flesh. But Sasha didn't think so.

One day a new Russian teacher came to our class. The people who stumbled into this job were quickly weeded out, and nothing helped, not even substantial hardship bonuses. This one was substituting for a teacher who'd been taken ill.

Dictation. All the pupils are sitting at their benches. Sasha is lying on the floor. Leaning on his bad arm and assiduously making large, ugly letters with his good one. His body is wracked by spasms, but he's making an honest effort.

"Excuse me, but could you dictate slower?"

"I'm dictating at the proper speed for a sixth-year class." Sasha smiles.

"You see, if I had hands like a sixth-year pupil, I wouldn't be bothering you."

"In that case, you should study in a special ed school."

Sasha doesn't take offense. He puts down his pen and reaches into his schoolbag for a book.

"What do you think you're doing?"

"Reading. I won't be able to write, and we're not allowed to bother the others doing an assignment."

"Stop that this instant."

"Will you dictate slower?"

Her patience snaps. This boy is nothing but a smart aleck. He could have just asked. In his situation, he can't be choosy, can he? He has to be punished. She spends a long time writing something in the classroom record.

"I'm going to call your parents in."

"From Leningrad? Mama won't come. At most, she'll call the director."

"Fine. Then I won't let you go to independent study and tomorrow you'll get a 'poor' in all your subjects."

That day she has evening duty.

The teacher is walking behind the attendants. The three sturdy women put Sasha in a wheelchair and try to take him back to the sleeping wing. He turns to the teacher:

"Why don't *you* take me back? Are you afraid you'll hurt yourself?"

And to the attendants:

"All right, girls, you have no choice, let's go."

He grabs one wheel of the chair with his good hand. His body is racked by spasms, and it hurts a lot, but there is virtually no way to detach his hand from the wheel's spokes. The attendants have to drag the chair with the locked wheel. They curse the teacher at the top of their lungs, but they drag the chair, swearing softly at Sasha.

And Sasha sings. He sings about a Russian ship that refused to surrender to the enemy's superior forces:

Our Varangian, *proud, shall never yield.*
And no man asks for mercy.

He's carted off to the sleeping wing and unloaded onto the floor. The teacher is happy. Sasha's 'poor' grades are a sure thing tomorrow.

That evening, after the children have eaten and the children's home workers are sitting down to their supper, Sasha crawls over to the school.

It's winter. It's snowing. It's late.

The school isn't far, a few hundred meters. He uses his good arm to rake the snow under him and cautiously shifts his bad arm. The worst part of it all is that the snow has melted just a little, and his bad arm keeps slipping on the icy asphalt, so he can't crawl very fast.

He's dressed like all us nonambulants. Leggings and a shirt, which is unbuttoned. He's not showing off, it's just that the shirt keeps slipping down one shoulder, and the buttons have come undone.

He crawls into the school building and then into his classroom and reads the textbooks for the next day.

The attendants discover the child is missing, follow his trail, and call for the teacher.

"Come sort this out with him yourself."

She walks into the classroom and takes a look at Sasha.

"What are you doing here?"

"I'm exercising my constitutional right. I'm doing my homework."

"But why did you crawl through the snow?"

"I didn't have any choice. I had to show you that you

can't conquer me with brute force. Yes, and see to some transportation because I'm not going to crawl back."

The teacher runs out. Later they told us she became hysterical and cried for a long time, but we didn't believe it. We didn't believe that teachers could cry over something that unimportant.

A few years later, I pay Sasha a visit.

"Mama, bring the vodka. Ruben and I are going to have a drink."

"But you didn't even drink at New Year's."

"New Year's comes every year, but I haven't seen Ruben for six."

We drink vodka and talk, and I ask him the crucial question.

"Sasha, are you glad the children's home was part of your life?"

"No. After the children's home I changed. I wish I'd never known it."

"But you had friends in the children's home. You met me."

Sasha thinks about that.

"Forgive me, Ruben. You're a fine fellow and my friend, and I'm glad I met you. But I wish there'd never been a children's home."

NEW YORK

The classroom supervisor is giving us political instruction again. We're being told about the horrors of the Western way of life. We're used to this, so nothing surprises us. I'm absolutely convinced that most people in America are living on the streets in cardboard boxes, that each and every American is building a bomb shelter, and that the country is experiencing crisis after crisis.

This time they're telling us about New York. They cite an article from the *New York Times* about free cheese being distributed to the unemployed. Several tons were handed out, one hundred grams per person. The teacher puts special emphasis on the fact that these poor folks won't get anything the next month.

I ask whether they won't starve to death then.

"Of course they will," the teacher replies. "But new crowds of fired workers will come to take their place."

I believe her.

We're alone in the classroom, the history teacher and I. He's writing something in the classroom record, and I'm reading.

He's sitting at the teacher's desk, and I'm lying on the floor nearby.

"Are you very busy?"

"What did you want?"

He looks up from his work. The teacher has very good and intelligent eyes and slightly graying hair. There's a pin on his jacket lapel.

"To ask a question."

"Ask away."

"In political instruction they were telling us that people in capitalist countries live in terrible poverty on the brink of starving to death. I was doing some figuring here, and everything tallies. They have billionaires in America, but very few. Right?"

"Right."

"They have millionaires too. Not many, but still lots more than billionaires. And there have to be many times more people of moderate means—shopkeepers and hairdressers—than there are millionaires. And many times more workers than shopkeepers. And many times more unemployed than workers. Right?"

"Right. That's no surprise. People there live very badly."

"You agree? Then according to my rough estimate, several hundred thousand unemployed people must be dying on the streets of New York, for instance, because they have nothing to eat. And that's not counting the workers starving to death. New York must be piled high with corpses! Someone has to keep clearing them out. I don't understand these Americans. Walking down the streets surrounded by people who are starving or starved to death. Why haven't they thrown out their landowners and capitalists yet?"

The teacher stands up, walks over, and squats in front of me. He gives me a strange look and smiles. He is almost laughing at my serious problem. He must just be in a very good mood today.

"How old are you?"

"You know, I'm ten."

"I know, I know," he says, now very cheerfully. "Isn't it a little early for you to be worrying about these things?"

I don't answer.

"Don't be angry. It's just a little too complicated for you."

The teacher stands up, takes the classroom record from the desk, and walks toward the door, where he turns around and gives me a serious, stern look, as if seeing me for the first time.

"Not a soul, you hear? Don't bring this topic up with a soul. You're a big boy now, you should understand."

The next day he comes over to me, bends down, and puts a big handsome book on the floor.

"Read this. It's a serious historical novel. I know you'll like it."

THE CUTLET

I obeyed my elders, I always obeyed my elders. At the end of every school year I was solemnly awarded an honorary certificate "for excellent study and exemplary behavior." I really was an excellent student, and the term "exemplary behavior" meant that I never argued with my teachers. It was easy to get along with the teachers; they were always going on about utter nonsense. They spent hours telling us completely unnecessary and pointless things, which we were supposed to recite in class. I have a good memory, and I had no trouble regurgitating the lessons. The teachers thought I was trying very hard. Strange people. I liked studying in school, where everything was for fun. They gave us books with pretty pictures and notebooks with either rules or grids. School was like a game. I played it with pleasure.

But I had to obey all my elders. The hardest was obeying the attendants. They didn't care what was written in smart books with pretty pictures. A Pushkin poem learned by heart or a mathematical formula didn't change anything. They demanded only one thing of me: that I ask for as little help as possible. From the time I was five years old they started telling me I was very heavy because I ate so much. "You keep gobbling away, and we have to carry you. You have no conscience. They gave birth to a Negro, and now we have to lug him around his whole life. Here's what, we foolish Russian women are good people, so we're putting up with this, we're taking care of him. But his parents were smart. They ran off to that Africa of theirs." And so it was, from one day to the next, I was constantly hearing about their goodness and compassion and about my black-skinned parents. It's a little funny, but I had to hear this same text in every institution in the Soviet Union—children's homes, hospitals, old folks' homes. It was as if they were reading it from some invisible, mysterious crib, like a homily, or a spell.

I tried the best I could. But the best I could do was to eat and drink less. I didn't know how to live without eating at all, and there was no one to ask. It didn't make sense to ask the teachers, because they weren't the real thing. They didn't have to bring the bedpans to us. I learned from the attendants that the teachers' job was much easier but their pay was higher. From the attendants' point of view, the teachers were being paid for doing nothing, and I fully agreed with the attendants. It's easy to tell stories from pretty books. Taking out the bedpans is hard work. That I understood very well.

But there was occasionally some use to be had from the teachers. Good teachers would bring me books and magazines from home. In one ladies' magazine I read about dieting. If you don't want to get fat, you have to cut meat and starch from your daily ration. I stopped eating bread and macaroni. They didn't treat us to meat very often, but occasionally they'd give us cutlets. It was hard to refuse cutlets, but I did, with the help of a smart book about secret agents. The book said that a real man has to exercise his willpower every day. So I did. At first I was really hungry, but then I got used to it. When they'd bring us our meal, I'd automatically pick out what I allowed myself to eat. Usually I limited myself to stewed fruit and a couple of spoonfuls of hot cereal. My mood improved. Now I was doing everything right, except that I was always sleepy, and by third period at school I couldn't think straight and my head spun. I fainted a few times right in class.

One day my stomach started to hurt and I didn't make it to the toilet in time. The attendant carried me there, put me on the floor, and started lecturing me. She yelled at me, told me how bad I was, and went on and on about the "black-assed bitch," and about how they all took such good care of me and I was so ungrateful. I didn't say anything. What was there to say? This wasn't the first time this had happened. It didn't make sense to cry and ask for her compassion because all my words fell apart against the sole argument—my soiled pants. She was yelling harder and harder, leaning over me, shaking her jowly cheeks, spraying spittle. I didn't say anything. What could I say? She was right. I was too fat and thought about food all the time. I was nearly eleven and I already weighed nearly seventeen kilos. I couldn't justify myself. I hated myself, too, for my weakness. Two days before I'd eaten a whole cutlet. I hadn't wanted to, I really hadn't. I thought I'd just sniff it, and then I took a bite. Before I knew it, I'd eaten the whole thing.

I didn't say anything. Then she grabbed my head with her greasy fingers and started jamming it into my dirty pants.

"Never says anything. If you'd just say something. Beg forgiveness, promise not to do it anymore. Just say something."

She was jamming my nose into my shit and repeating

very softly: "Say it, say it, say it." What could I say? I knew perfectly well that what they needed from me had nothing to do with words. I'd already tried all the words. The attendant wanted, she really wanted just one thing: for me to learn how to go to the toilet by myself. That was a promise I couldn't make, and therefore I didn't say anything.

"Say it, say it, say it. Are you going to say it? Are you?" she kept repeating in a monotone. "Say it, say it." It was like the film about the war where the German officer was interrogating the brave Russian spy. A German officer. A German.

All of a sudden a simple German sentence came out of me: *"Russische schwein."*

"Du bist Russische schwein," I shouted in desperate impudence. *"Du bist Russische schwein. Russische schwein. Russische schwein. Russische schwein.* The Germans were right to shoot your parents. They should have shot you too."

It was words, nothing but words. But they were effective. The woman lost it. As a child she had lived through the German occupation and the postwar famine. I knew I was hitting her where it hurt.

I'm used to my disability. Only sometimes, for a minute, an insurmountable desire to stand on my own two feet bubbles up. This desire usually bubbles up spontaneously, from deep down in my animal core. At that moment I had a very strong urge to pick up a sharp knife in my right hand and shove the blade into her fat belly. And shove and shove. To disembowel her. I wanted revenge.

I began to cry. I was crying and shouting. I was shouting unfair and awful things into the face of this foolish woman. I was shouting obscenities and trying to wound her as badly as I could.

A teacher was walking by. She came in at my shouting and saw me lying naked on the cement floor in shit and tears. She understood immediately and raised a hue and cry. Good grown-ups washed me and carried me to my bed. The nurse came with an injection.

"Calm down, little boy. Everything's going to be all right. I'm going to give you a nice shot now and you'll fall asleep."

"Get away from me, you bitch, you slut! You're a Russian. I hate you. I hate all Russians. Fascists, swine. A nice little shot? Let's have a shot, only not that one, a real one, so that I die for good. I'm black-assed and you're Russians. Kill me then and stop torturing me. You won't even waste your poison on me. You're worse than the Fascists. The Fascists killed all the disabled people, but you just humiliate me."

They gave me the shot. I hollered and hollered. I told them everything: about the diet, about being fat. I promised them I wouldn't eat anything anymore. The teacher and nurse listened to me but didn't understand. They tried to calm me down.

The shot worked. I fell asleep quickly and slept through to midday. I felt better. Calm. At mess they gave me a cutlet. I decided to eat everything. I ate the cutlet, the borscht, and the bread. So what if I got fat? I didn't care anymore.

THE GERMAN

He came into our classroom with a quick, mincing step, pulled out his chair, and sat down. Without looking at us, he began reciting poetry, loudly and clearly. He recited for a long time, then stood up and surveyed the class.

"That was Goethe. I was reciting in German. Maybe one day you'll be able to read Goethe in the original. I'm your new foreign-language teacher."

He walked over to the desk and opened the textbook.

"First of all, I must apologize to Ruben. Ruben, I'm very sorry I can't teach you Spanish. I don't know Spanish. Study German for now. If you learn German, you can learn any other language. Remember that."

I did.

A peculiar teacher, very peculiar. Every once in a while he'd get carried away in the middle of a lesson and recite poetry for a long time. He got very excited and lively telling us about Germany. He radiated joy when the German soccer team won a match. He considered everything German the best. A real teacher—screwy and fanatic.

———

The German lesson. Our class is all worked up and we're arguing with the teacher. The topic of our argument—Germany's superiority—never changed. You could argue about anything you liked except Germany's defeat in the Second World War. If you mentioned the war, the teacher stopped talking and started wiping his glasses fussily and in a dry, colorless voice would tell us to open our textbooks to a specific page and recite those endless German verbs.

His eyes are burning and his cheeks are red. He is triumphantly tossing out to the class the names of German composers, philosophers, and poets. He's practically shouting about the superiority of German shipwrights. He's happy, pleased. There's nothing we can say. We move on to a discussion of agriculture. We listen ecstatically to what he says about centners and hectares, the production volumes and incredible harvests.

It's all spoiled by someone's timid question:

"What about figs?"

"What figs?"

"Do they grow figs in Germany?"

He droops. His mood is ruined. We recite those endless German verbs.

He comes over to me and sits down. He's holding a little brown bag of figs.

"Want some?"

"Thank you."

We eat the figs in silence. We finish. He rises heavily from the floor, brushes off his pants, and sighs.

"But figs don't grow in Germany. That's the truth. They don't grow there at all."

MUSIC

The music wasn't ours. It was someone else's. It had been recorded on X-ray film. The children's-home workers brought in blank X-ray film from their endless visits to hospitals and exchanged it for recorded tapes at a rate of one for two. It was a business.

The innocuous Western hits horrified our teachers.

"Do you know what they're singing about?"

We didn't. They took the music away, the transgressors' behavior was discussed by the school's pedagogical council, and a struggle against the capitalist influence went into full swing. A pointless struggle.

The boys started wearing their hair long. Instructions were sent from Moscow on how to fight this "contagion." The pupils' hair was not supposed to fall below mid-ear. Ears were measured with a ruler and their midpoints gauged by eye. There was an unending struggle for the right to have your hair be a little bit snazzier than your friend's.

The arguments over long hair didn't concern me. They always shaved my head, because I wasn't an ambulant.

I really wanted to find out what the people on the records were singing about. I wanted to learn their language.

THE LETTER

It was a bad children's home, a very bad children's home. The food was bad and the grown-ups were bad. Everything was bad. Like prisons, children's homes vary. This one was particularly bad. Hardest of all to bear was the cold, because the home wasn't heated. This was especially hard in winter. The ink froze in our pens. It was cold in the classrooms and cold in the sleeping wing—no matter where I crawled, it was cold. In other children's homes, it was only cold in the halls, but in this one it was cold everywhere. In other children's homes, even in the halls you could crawl over to the radiator, but this unit had nothing but useless pieces of cold metal inside. A bad children's home, a very bad children's home.

They brought in a new kid. Cerebral palsy. The boy was very big and strong and he writhed with strong, constant spasms. Spasms like that are rare. The attendants took him by the arm, led him to the sleeping wing, and put him on his bed.

His face was contorted and his speech unintelligible, or nearly unintelligible. I understood everything. He wasn't very smart, but he wasn't a complete moron, which was what everyone, from his teachers to the other kids, considered him.

He sat on his bed continuously repeating a strange sound—a birdlike screech, *klsk, klsk*—like an incantation. There are no words in Russian made up entirely of consonants. I knew that, and read the vowels on his lips, or rather, from the movement of his facial muscles. The boy wasn't crazy. Day and night he was repeating a simple word: *kolyaska*. Wheelchair. It would have been hard to call him normal. He still didn't understand, he didn't understand anything. There wasn't anything to eat at that children's home, so there certainly weren't any wheelchairs.

The children in the home had the right to correspond with their parents. Every week the aide urged the children to write letters. And every week the children stubbornly refused to write home. Foolish children. They were given a free envelope and a blank sheet of paper.

In the younger classes nearly everyone wrote letters. The pages with the childish scrawl were handed in to the aide, who corrected their grammatical errors, put the letters into the envelopes, and mailed them. Everyone knew exactly what you were supposed to write in letters. Everyone wrote about their grades, the concerned adults, their friendly class. Every holiday, the children were given pretty cards, all identical, for sending greetings to their parents. The adults especially liked the cards. Every card had to be ruled off in pencil, and then a draft was written of the greeting text. The aide would correct the mistakes in the draft. Then you could rewrite the text into the card in pencil, and after that, if it had been written without a mistake, go over the pencil with colored ink. Everyone also knew what you couldn't write about. You couldn't write about anything bad. For instance, you weren't allowed to write about the food. Especially the food. But in their own letters, the foolish parents for some reason always asked specifically about the food. Therefore all the letters frequently began with a standard "Dear Mama, They're feeding us well." The children were praised for good letters and yelled at for bad ones. The especially bad letters were read out loud to the entire class.

The upperclassmen didn't write letters. Their parents were well aware of what a children's home was. Why cause them unnecessary worry? And if someone did have to write a letter, he could always buy an envelope, assuming he had the money. It was only the dull children who gave their letters to the aide. Everyone knew that according to regulations she was supposed to take the letter home, read it, and only then decide whether to send it or not. But any adult could drop a letter in a mailbox. Usually the children asked the attendants for this simple favor, but one boy took advantage of the bread-truck drivers. Bread was brought to the children's home every day. He would approach the driver and whisper: "Please drop this letter in a mailbox." The driver would look around, take the letter without saying a word, and get into his truck. This boy's letters were sent that very day; his parents knew it from the postmark. The boy tried proudly to convince us that all truck drivers were good people. His papa was a truck driver.

The aide may actually have believed that the older students didn't write letters. Or she might have suspected something when, once a week, she urged everyone to write. She would talk and no one would say a word. That was the drill. If the aide put special pressure on one of the students, the fellow would have to pretend he'd decided to write a letter. He'd write quickly on the sheet of paper, "The pearl barley is fucking fantastic," slip the page in the envelope, and seal the envelope with the glue we used to make airplane models. Not a single letter like that ever reached its intended recipient—not that it needed to. On the other hand, no one bothered its writer again.

The new kid sat on his bed all the time, shouting and crying. At first the attendants treated him all right. In the morning they took him off his bed, set him on the floor, and asked him how to put him down so he could crawl. The handicapped boy lay on his back, his arms and legs jerking in the air, and bellowed something indecipherable. When they turned him over on his stomach, he shouted even harder. The attendants put him back on his bed and left. What else could they do?

He shouted and bellowed and cried. Day and night. At first his classmates felt like beating him to get him to shut up, but they didn't. Retards didn't get beaten up. The guys just asked the administration to move him to a different ward. No one wanted to sleep to his nocturnal shouting. While the adults were trying to figure out where to put the unfortunate boy, the guys tried to entertain the little fool. They brought him balls and children's toys, but nothing helped. The guys refused to give up. He had to like something. Someone offered him a notebook, a fat notebook with grid-lined paper. The little fool was overjoyed and nodded. He grabbed the notebook, calmed down, and suddenly said quite clearly: "Give." His unexpected success cheered everyone up. They asked him to say "give" over and over. He would repeat it and smile. The word "give" came out well for him. He could pronounce the words "mama," "papa," "give," and "yes" clearly and almost fluently. He had trouble with "no." It started with an almost inaudible "n," followed by a pause and then a long "o-o-o." But that was enough. He asked for a pen. They gave him a pen and, without him asking, a table, which they moved close to his bed. They put the pen on the table. He froze for a moment, picked up the pen with his surprisingly deft right hand, stretched out confidently across the table, holding the notebook steady beneath him, opened the notebook with his chin, and jabbed the pen at the blank page. He sat up: his outflung arms twitched pointlessly, and his legs under the table beat an arrhythmic tattoo. He laughed, and the guys laughed with him.

The new kid's life changed. He slept soundly at night, and in the morning an attendant stuck a pen in his hand and put the notebook in front of him. He sat on the bed all day, falling on the notebook with his whole body, trying over and over to jab the pen onto the blank page, then straightening up, laughing joyfully, admiring his drawings. For two weeks, the guys in the ward slept peacefully. For two weeks, the little fool patiently scratched his bizarre squiggles and purposeful designs—shapes and signs he alone could make out—in the notebook. When there was no blank space left in the notebook, he gave a shout. He gave another shout. Notebooks were prized in the children's home, especially grid-ruled ones. But the little fool wanted to draw and the guys wanted to sleep at night. They bought him a new one. Let him draw. He didn't even look at the fresh notebook. He threw the pen on the floor, put the old notebook—a crumpled, useless toy, now—next to him on the bed, and shouted.

Now everyone understood what he was shouting. He was shouting "Mama." He was shouting loudly. By now the guys were fairly used to his way of talking. Everyone tried to get out of him what he still needed, to convince him to stop

shouting. They promised to bring him many more note-books, but nothing helped. They said one word after another to him, to each of which he said "no." Then they started naming letters. They were just running through the alphabet, and if he liked a letter he'd say "yes." What formed was the word "send." That cleared things up. He wanted his drawings sent to his mama. They called the aide in, and she examined the notebook for a long time. The crumpled pages were covered solid with symbols of some kind. In one place the symbols would be random and in another clustered thickly in an indistinguishable clump of inky interweavings. Some pages were covered with solid circles. The circles were of different sizes and not always closed. Only at a stretch would you take them for the letter *O*. But who would draw the letter *O* on two pages in a row?

The aide refused to send the notebook to his parents. It's a letter, she said, and I have to know its content. A scandal was brewing. What content could there be in his clumsy scrawls? The strict teacher got to go home after her shift and get a good night's sleep, while the guys were again being kept awake by this little fool's shouts. How fair was that? The aide had to find a solution to their troubles right away. She went over to the new kid.

"Is this a letter?"

"No."

"Are these your drawings?"

"Yes."

"Do you want me to send them to your mama?"

"Yes."

"What if we don't send your mama the whole notebook? What if we choose the prettiest drawings and send them?"

"No. No."

He said "no"—a word that was very hard for him—twice. Then he started shouting. He shouted "Mama," stamped his feet, and tried to say "no" once more. He couldn't.

"Fine, fine. I understand everything. Your mama likes it a lot when you draw. I'll send her all your drawings. I'll write a letter to your mama. I'll write her that you like it here very much, you have a lot of friends, and you love to draw. You do like it here with us, don't you?"

"Yes."

So they had their talk. The aide sent the new kid's notebook to his parents. The new kid calmed down. He slept at night and sat on his bed during the day, staring at a fixed point.

A month later they brought wheelchairs to the children's home. There were a lot of wheelchairs, enough for everyone. They gave the new kid a wheelchair, too. The attendants picked him up under the arms and he stood. They led him to the wheelchair and he sat down. They tried to put his feet on the rests, but he wouldn't let them. They took the footrests off. He pushed off with his feet and he was on his way. He picked up speed very quickly with his strong legs and rolled down the hallway.

At the next assembly the aide yelled at the new kid. She said the same foolish things she usually did in these cases. How the country was bending over backward to give us its last crust of bread and how ungrateful he was. She tried to argue that she had treated the new kid like a human being and sent his parents his notebook, but in the notebook, it turns out, he had slung mud over the entire collective of the children's home and painted life in the home in the blackest colors and found fault with the pedagogical council and the staff for no reason at all. She went on and on and on. The new kid wasn't listening. When she got as far as the typical accusations of callousness and heartlessness, he pushed away from his desk and rolled out into the hallway.

They didn't let him write any more letters. Not that he asked. After lessons he would roll up and down the hallway and play with balls for hours. He regularly asked for seconds at mess. He had to be spoon-fed, and the attendants didn't want to feed him seconds. They tried to explain all this to him, but in vain. He would ride after an attendant in his wheelchair until she relented. The attendants would go to their room to hide from his pestering. He would sit outside the door and shout. When everyone was exasperated, they would come out of the room and give him another plate of soup or hot cereal. Gradually everyone got used to him, and they always gave him seconds so that the pesky invalid would leave them in peace.

When he and I were alone, we'd talk. Slowly pronouncing each word, he would say a sentence and watch me warily. I would repeat what he'd said. Gradually he began to trust me, and I didn't need to repeat what he'd said anymore. We just talked. I asked him what exactly had been in that letter.

"Ruben. I thought a lot."

"I know you thought a lot and you wrote a fine letter. What did you write?"

"MAMA, THEY FEED ME BADLY AND WON'T GIVE ME A CHAIR."

By "chair" he'd meant a wheelchair.

The entire first page of the first letter he'd written in his life had been covered with the letter *M*. Uppercase and lowercase. He had hoped that at least one letter on the whole page would be understood. Sometimes one letter took up several pages. The thick notebook, ninety-six pages, had been completely filled.

"The first four letters were unnecessary," I tried to argue.

"I thought a long time."

"But the first four letters were unnecessary anyway. You might not have had enough room in the notebook."

He thought about that. Then he smiled broadly and said slowly and very clearly: "Ma-ma."

PIROZHKI

A children's home, a home for children. Where children are prepared for their future, their adult life. In addition to general education subjects, in a children's home they teach the basics of survival for the complicated world that begins outside the school gate. The boys are taught to understand wiring, to use a fret-saw, and to assemble and repair furniture; the girls learn to sew, knit, and cook. It's not so easy, teaching a boy without hands to change electrical plugs, and teaching a one-armed girl to knit seems almost impossible. It's hard. Really, it's very hard. Our teachers were able to accomplish things the parents of a disabled child couldn't even imagine.

I'm lying on the classroom floor. A girl comes in carrying a tray. In place of one leg she has a prosthesis, but by our children's-home measures, she's practically healthy. On the tray are pirozhki. Hot and golden.

"Where are the boys?" she says. "We girls baked pirozhki, and they promised to stop by the kitchen and taste them."

"They went to the movies."

"What do you mean, the movies?"

"They got taken to the movies today. Tomorrow they'll take you. You see, you have cooking class."

"But why didn't they tell us? What are we supposed to do with the pirozhki now?"

She puts the tray on the teacher's desk, sits down at a bench, takes a pirozhok from the tray, and hands it to me. A pirozhok with potatoes and onion. I'm eating a pirozhok.

"It's delicious," I say. "Your pirozhki came out fine."

The girl doesn't hear me. She's staring off into space.

"That's odd . . . Where are the boys?"

THE FIGHT

Fights were a rarity in the children's home. When we did fight, though, we fought cruelly. We fought by the rules. Only scum bit or pulled hair, and knives and brass knuckles were off-limits for us. If the disabilities were unequal, vengeance was allowed. There were no expiration dates on vengeance. I knew a guy who proudly described how he'd pushed his offender under a car for an insult inflicted a year and a half earlier. He hadn't done a very good job of it, though. The car was just getting going and the boy wasn't hit hard. At the evening gathering the avenger was vindicated. He had only one arm, and the boy he'd pushed had two arms and a leg. It was all fair and square. A fight would have been impossible. The one-armed boy had taken his revenge—that is, he had acted properly. When his victim was discharged from the hospital, the two even became friends. Strength was respected. Everyone had the right to be strong.

I loved autumn. In the autumn, the happy few who were taken home for the summer vacations returned. The autumn was noisy and fun, and there was a lot of delicious food and interesting talk about home, the summer, and parents.

I always hated spring. I still do. In the spring my best friends went away for vacation. Every spring, we hoped that this year someone would be taken home who had not been the year before. Everyone had hopes—even those whose parents lived too far away, even the orphans. We would try to spend most of the day in the schoolyard, near the gate. We didn't talk about it, we just waited. We just hoped. I never hoped, because I knew that no one would ever come for me.

That autumn Seryoga returned unhappy. It was odd seeing a sad Seryoga. Of course, everyone was a little sad after vacation, and everyone missed home. But their sadness was relieved by seeing their friends, by new impressions and new textbooks. We'd moved up a grade, we were older.

Seryoga, an overgrown, legless fellow, came to see us in our ward on his trolley. He wanted to consult with the lads. He spoke mainly with Genka.

"I'm going to have to fight."

"Seryoga, you're the strongest boy in the home. Everyone knows that. Who would ever fight you?"

"That's just the point. It's not in the home, it's there, on the outside."

"What's the fight about?"

"A woman. They said they'd drive me to my grave, dig me into the ground. The day before I left to come back here. They said if I showed up next spring they'd kill me."

Everyone knew that Seryoga had a girl waiting for him on the outside. A healthy girl. A normal, pretty girl. Our girls didn't even attempt to flirt with him. They knew that when Seryoga finished school he'd marry his girlfriend.

Genka didn't ask about the woman. That just wasn't

done. If the guy wanted to, he'd tell us himself. If he didn't, that was his business.

"I don't know what to tell you. I've never been on the outside. Is he strong?"

"Of course. And a year older than me. He goes to vocational school."

"Then it's curtains for you. He'll kill you. He'll give you a good kick and trample you to death."

"I know that. But I have to fight."

Genka pondered this. There was no one smarter than Genka in the children's home. And Genka knew it. It's very hard to hide the truth in a children's home. Everybody knows everything about everyone. We knew who was the strongest in the home and which class the prettiest girl was in.

"You know, Seryoga, I think you have a chance. A small one, but a chance. You have to knock him down. If he falls—throw yourself on top of him and smother him. He's two legs bigger than you, so he's stronger. You don't have any other option."

Seryoga knew he had no other option. From that day on he started working out. That year everyone was working out. They set up horizontal bars in the schoolyard, and the electrician and phys ed teacher slapped together a few primitive weight benches out of metal pipes. There were a lot fewer drinking parties. The teachers were happy because the children spent nearly all their free time in the schoolyard. Seryoga, an influential fellow, quit smoking, and so did the others who'd decided to work out. True, later lots of them broke down and started up again. But not Seryoga.

Every day. An hour in the morning, two hours in the

evening, and four hours each on Saturday and Sunday. For the nine months of the school year the children's home worked out.

Those who were missing an arm worked the muscles of the one they had. All of a sudden they started wearing their prostheses. The formerly useless plastic imitation arms did indeed become essential. Each boy would fill his prosthesis with pig iron, depending on how much training he was doing, so he wouldn't pull his back out or twist his spine favoring his good side. Meanwhile, the prosthesis itself wasn't a bad weapon in a fight.

There was one armless fellow in the children's home. He didn't have any arms at all. Those who were just missing hands could develop their stumps for fighting with prostheses. But his prostheses, useless toys, only got in his way, so he didn't wear them at all. He worked out more than anyone else, even more than Seryoga. He would sit on a stool, hook his feet under a cupboard, and lean back, touching the floor with the top of his head. He was always working out, even while he did homework. He would memorize poems and repeat the material they'd gone over in class, working out all the while, and he said that he remembered everything better that way. In the evenings he would spend a long time striking his heels against a stack of newspapers he'd hung on the wall. He would jump, strike the newspapers with his heel, jump back, and strike again. Every day, he proudly tore one newspaper from the stack with his teeth. One day when the newspaper stack on the wall had grown noticeably thinner, during yet another training session, paint started flaking off the wall and the stack tore off its nail. He kept striking his heels furiously against the bare brick. The adults came and painted the wall, but they didn't yell at him because they realized he hadn't done it on purpose. They laughed, advising him to train on the concrete wall of the garage. The armless boy would wake up before everyone else, go outside, and hammer away at the blameless concrete wall. Now he could train his legs in the mornings, too, without disturbing the others' sleep. A strong fellow.

Seryoga did have arms. He was developing his physique the usual way. Except that when he did chin-ups on the bar, he wore a backpack. At first the backpack held only a small weight, to compensate for the weight of his missing legs, but then Seryoga started adding dumbbells. Even wearing a heavy backpack, though, he could do more than forty chin-ups in a set.

Even the phys ed teacher liked the backpack idea. He started coming to workouts with one, too. Leading the children in morning exercises was part of the phys ed teacher's duties. Before, hardly anyone had gone to his class. That year, though, the phys ed instructor became the most important teacher in the school, even more important than the math teacher. He helped the guys a lot and came up with training ideas for the disabled. He warned us about overdoing it and gave us long lectures on anatomy. A fine teacher.

Seryoga's "pushers" were his pride and joy. "Pushers" was our name for the small boards with handles that the legless invalids used to push off as they wheeled around on their trolleys. Seryoga smelted his pushers himself, in shop class, from aluminum tubes. These aluminum pushers with their rubber treads didn't stay light for long, though. Every evening Seryoga would light a small fire in the schoolyard, smelt some pig iron, and pour a little into his pushers. Every day, the pushers got heavier and heavier. He used them as usual. As always, he wheeled around the children's home on his trolley, only now he always had convenient dumbbells at hand. By spring, each pusher weighed exactly five kilos. Seryoga decided to stop at five.

When summer vacation came around we gave Seryoga a very quiet sendoff. We could see that over the winter months of training Seryoga had become very strong, but that meant absolutely nothing. Every time Seryoga reached any milestone, we realized that it was still too little, much too little. Seryoga worked out every day, but it was absolutely clear that somewhere out there, in his hometown, his enemy was working out, too, exercising every muscle of his intact body. When Seryoga managed to do fifty chin-ups for the first time, we were sure that his rival had done at least a hundred. If Seryoga pressed the dumbbell eight times with his left arm, his rival did it more like twenty times.

The summer passed quickly. One more children's-home summer. In the autumn, as always, the parents brought their children back to the home. They brought Seryoga, too. No one asked about the fight, and Seryoga didn't say anything. Not until one day, when Seryoga came to see the lads again and Genka asked him, hinted at it, really. Said something vague about summer vacation. Seryoga understood right away but got embarrassed and looked down. It was awkward refusing Genka.

"There wasn't any fight," Seryoga said softly. "There wasn't. The first night I got home I found him. He and some other guy were standing around smoking. I asked him if he remembered me, and he said he did. Then I swung my pusher at his knee with all my might. His leg broke and bent backward.

He fell down. He started shouting out, starting calling for his mama. I punched him in the gut a couple of times. He got hoarse. I turned around to face his friend, thinking I'd have to fight both of them, but his friend had already run off to call the grown-ups. Stoolie. They ran up and called for the doctor. They asked me how I'd done that to him and I said I'd used my hands. There was a big fuss. He really had had a knife in his pocket."

"Then what?"

"Then nothing. His father came over to our house. We sat down and had a drink. I told his father the whole story. And then that guy and I got to know each other. He's an okay guy, just weak. He went around on crutches all summer. It's strange. I invited him to come fishing, and he said he wasn't allowed to go far on crutches. He's got strange parents, too. I tried to explain to them that half our children's home goes around on crutches, but they didn't understand. And the fishing was good this summer. I caught a pike. Good fishing."

That evening the lads argued for a long time. They just couldn't understand why that fellow with the broken leg hadn't fought. After all, he still had two whole arms and a good leg left, and he even had a knife in his pocket. He was a strange one, and so was his friend.

THE BICYCLE

Lights-out. The grown-ups turn off the lights and leave. The children are supposed to go to sleep. The best time of the day is the couple of hours after lights-out. We're not sleepy. It's dark. If there's no holiday, there's no reason to turn on the light. A holiday is another matter. On a holiday you can open cans of food you've stashed away, drink some wine, and if there isn't any wine, at least tea. If it isn't a holiday and you're not sleepy, you can talk. At night you can talk about anything you like and no one's going to laugh at you. At night you can think about home, your mama and papa. At night— you can. No one's going to say you're a weakling or a mama's boy. At night—they won't.

That night they were talking about their parents. I said nothing. Usually, when they ran out of things to talk about they would ask me to tell them something interesting from a book I'd read. That night I didn't have anything to say. I just listened.

As they did nearly every autumn, the boys were arguing over who had the best parents. Naturally, they all had fine parents. The best mamas in the world, the strongest papas. Not everyone had a papa. Those who did had the very, very best.

"I have a great papa," one fellow began. "The very best."

"Weren't you telling us how he drinks?"

"So what if he does? He's still great. This summer our neighbor gave his son a bicycle for his birthday. A grown-up bicycle, a two-wheeler. He let everyone take a ride. Everyone in our yard took turns taking rides on the bicycle. My papa didn't drink for three days. He was thinking. He went around the house in a foul mood. Mama bought him beer, but he wouldn't even drink beer. He picked up my notebook and pen and did some figuring. He went to the bookkeeper and then to the trade union committee. On Saturday, he went to the district center and came back sober. He'd brought me a receiver. Here, he says, that neighbor of mine can only buy his son a bicycle on his birthday, but I can buy my family presents whenever I want. For two weeks he didn't drink. He asked to work the night shift, to make more money. It's a big radio, an expensive one. No one we know has anything like it. It has all the countries of the world written on the dial. You can pick up anything you want on it. Music, children's shows. There's even a show where they read books for the blind. I listened to it every day. A fine radio. And my neighbor's bicycle broke pretty soon anyway. I've got a smart papa. He knows what to buy. A radio is better than a bicycle, after all. Right?"

No one even bothered to argue. It was obvious. A radio is a serious thing, whereas a bicycle . . . What's a bicycle? A hunk of steel with two wheels. That's all.

THE SPANISH GIRL

The hospital. I'm lying here in a cast to my waist. I'm lying on my back. I've been lying here for more than a year. I'm looking at the ceiling. I've been looking at the same spot on the ceiling for more than a year. I have no desire to live. I'm trying to eat and drink as little as possible. I'm making an honest effort. I'm trying because I know that the less often you eat the less often you have to ask for help. Asking others for help is the most terrible and unpleasant thing in life.

Rounds. The doctor is going from ward to ward with an entourage of very young students. He gets to my bed. He glances at my chart and recites what I've been hearing for a year. He talks about my arms and legs and my mental retardation. I'm used to it. They do rounds frequently. I've grown used to a lot in this hospital. I almost don't care.

The doctor pulls back the sheet, takes out his pointer, and spends a long and tedious time showing the bored students my body. Explaining to them the methods of treatment and other nonsense. The students are practically asleep.

"How much is two plus two?" he asks me suddenly.

"Four."

"And three plus three?"

"Six."

The students rouse, wake up almost. The doctor is explaining to them briefly and convincingly that not all the parts of my brain have been affected. "The boy even remembers his name and recognizes his doctors." He smiles at me. I know those kinds of smiles and I hate them. It's the way people smile at very small children or animals. Insincerely.

"And how much is two times two?"

He puts special stress on the word *times*. This is too much. Even for me, this is too much. Even in this hospital, damn it.

"Two times two is four, three times three is nine, four times four is sixteen. I'm cold. Pull the sheet over me or at least close the windowpane. Yes, I'm retarded, I know that, but retarded people get cold, too. I'm not your guinea pig."

I'd heard the term *guinea pig* when they were redoing my cast. The doctor looks at me very strangely. He stands there. In silence. A girl from his entourage quickly reaches toward me, pulls the sheet up, and just as quickly walks away.

Rounds are over.

That evening, a woman in street clothes comes to see me. She's young and beautiful. She's not wearing a lab coat. I haven't seen anyone without a lab coat for more than a year. She leans toward me decisively and asks:

"Are you Spanish?"

"Yes."

"I'm Spanish, too. I'm studying at the teachers' institute. They asked us to retell the *Lay of Igor's Campaign*. It's a hard text, and I don't understand any of it. Can you help me?"

"But I'm still little, and you're studying at the institute."

"That doesn't matter."

"Okay, I'll try to help you."

She takes the book out of her bag, pulls a chair over to my bed, and reads. She reads slowly, almost syllable by syllable. I know most of the "incomprehensible" words, and there are handy notes in the book for the ones I don't. A fine book.

It's getting dark. She has to go. She closes the book and stands up.

"We still haven't gone through it all. I'll come back tomorrow. My name is Lolita."

"Mine is Ruben."

She smiles.

"I know your name. I'll come tomorrow, Ruben."

That night I can hardly sleep. No one has ever come to see me before. Nearly everyone has someone on the outside: parents, grandmothers and grandfathers, brothers and sisters. One Georgian fellow even had a visit from his cousin. His parents are dead and he's being raised by his uncle. The Georgian explained to me that his cousin was his blood relative. And a blood relative, he told me, is the closest person on earth. He has lots of blood relatives. I don't have anyone.

The next day the volunteers came to see us. The teachers' institute had suddenly adopted the children's wing of our hospital for their volunteer project. That is, they'd probably had it formally before, but this time they came to our ward specifically. Among them, naturally, was Lolita. She had on a white coat over her dress.

She walked over to my bed.

"See? I came. Why are you crying?"

The volunteers came often, almost every Sunday. Lolita wasn't always with them, but when she was, she would spend a long time sitting by my bed. We talked. Just shot the breeze. Talking with a human being meant a lot to me, too much for a child's psyche. An enchanting luxury. For her it was always too little. Just coming to see a sick, lonely child was too little. One time the students brought a movie projector to the hospital. They showed cartoons in the lounge; as always, I stayed in my room alone. Lolita came in, took a look at me, said something, and I said something back. She must be in a bad mood today, I thought. She quickly ran out of the room. The next Sunday the students brought the projector into my room. They turned my bed sideways to face the wall. In a bright spot on the hospital wall, a funny wolf kept trying to catch a crafty rabbit. All ten installments, ten installments of the most famous Russian cartoon of all. I was seeing this cartoon for the first time in my life.

With Lolita, everything was for the first time. For the first time, they moved me from the bed to a stretcher and took me outside. For the first time in my entire hospital life I could see the sky. The sky, instead of the eternal white ceiling.

It was a holiday. A holiday in the hospital. Holidays didn't concern me. I didn't care about holidays. Someone somewhere else was having a good time.

A very beautiful, brightly made-up Lolita ran into the ward wearing a Spanish costume and without her lab coat.

"Come on, Ruben, they're bringing the stretcher and we're taking you to the lounge. Today I'm going to dance!"

She was beautiful and filled with joy. A walking, talking holiday.

A nurse came into the room. A regular nurse in a white coat.

"You can't move the patient. They operated on him recently."

Lolita's arrival had made me forget all about my operation. Once again the doctors had cut off my casts. More pointless pain. I couldn't. I could never do anything. Actually, I was used to it, I was almost used to the eternal *can't.* Lolita wasn't. She ran out of the room. She left.

A couple of minutes later, some people ran in noisily and started speaking Spanish—Lolita, one Pablo, and a short fellow with a mustache. Pablo had his guitar. I knew Pablo. The one with the mustache switched to Russian.

"You're supposed to be at the event, immediately."

"I'm going to dance here. Here and now."

"You're going to dance there, where they tell you. I'm taking my guitar. Pablo, let's go."

"Are you going, Pablo?"

Lolita gave the grown fellow a provocative look. It was an open look that held a challenge, and joy. Pablo looked down.

The fellow with the mustache left, leading away the unhappy Pablo. We were all alone in the hospital room.

Lolita danced. She danced, snapping out the rhythm with her fingers.

Lolita danced. She danced for herself. Intensely and strictly she tapped out the strange, exotic melody. Without a guitar and without Pablo. She danced for real, every part of her.

Dance collectives sometimes came to the children's home. The young fools would stamp earnestly on the stage of the children's-home club. The master of ceremonies would come out on stage and announce another number and the fools would stamp on the stage differently. It was boring.

Only once was the established order violated. Yet another dance group had come to visit us on Victory Day. For the umpteenth time they cranked up the usual music. Suddenly our history teacher dashed out on stage and whispered something in the ear of the distraught accordionist. The teacher began to dance, squatting and kicking and jangling his medals. The girls stepped back for this war veteran and stayed out of his way. The man had been drinking, so let him dance. The teacher had indeed had a little to drink that day. That's what Victory Day was for. He danced well, with abandon. His performance seemed curiously intimate. He radiated freedom and strength. I never saw him like that again.

But now I'd seen real live dancing for the first time, in a northern Russian hospital. Real dancing. Spanish dancing.

We said good-bye. Lolita had to go away.

"I'll find you, little boy. I will definitely write you a letter, so wait for it."

She promised to write, but I had no faith in her. Once again, I had no faith.

"You won't be able to find me. I don't even know what home they're going to take me to."

I had no faith.

A couple of years later a letter did arrive. A regular letter. The first letter I'd ever got in my life. In it was a beautiful card. On it was a Spanish girl dancing in a colorful dress. The dress on the card was decorated with colored threads. They didn't make cards like that in Russia.

The teacher gave me the letter. She put the open envelope in front of me. She sat down facing me.

"Ruben. You and I have to have a serious talk. I read the

letter. There's nothing dangerous in it. Not yet. I hope you realize you can't write an answer. Spain is a capitalist country. Corresponding with capitalist countries is not recommended. Any foreigner could turn out to be a spy. You're a smart boy and you have to understand that the children's-home administration does not have the right to subject you to a risk like that."

She took the envelope away and left.

I looked at the card for a long time. Then I hid it in my math textbook.

The next morning my card was gone.

THE VOLGA

The Volga. The great Russian river. There's a car called a Volga, too. There are many kinds of cars. When I was little, I thought there were only Volgas, Moskviches, and Zaporozhetses. They wrote about other cars in books, but I'd never seen other cars.

Each year, in May, the children's home held a graduation party and invited graduates from previous years. Many of these former students came in cars. The teachers greeted them and were happy to see all of them, even the ones who came in "handicap" cars—cycle-cars with moped engines. They were especially happy to see the ones who came in Volgas. Volgas are expensive. If a former pupil bought a Volga, he became special. At the ceremony he was invited onto the stage and asked to deliver a commencement speech to the graduates.

Sometimes we talked about cars. The children argued over whose papa had the coolest car. Not all parents had cars. Far from it. Some had motorcycles at home. Motorcycles didn't rate in our debates. Cars did, including the cars owned by grandfathers or older brothers. One boy didn't have a papa, but his mama had a car. He was very proud of his mama and her car. If someone's parents didn't live too far away and they came to the children's home in their own car, there was nothing to prove. It was harder for a boy who lived far away. He could show a photograph of the whole family in front of the car, of course. But who was going to take a photograph at face value? If his papa mentioned the car in a letter, that was another matter. If his parents wrote that the car had a flat tire, that meant they had a car. Parents wouldn't lie. Why should they?

I didn't know at the time whether my papa had a car. I still don't. If we ever meet, I'll ask. I didn't know at the time that I had the best grandfather in the world. The very best. That my grandfather was the general secretary of the Communist Party. I didn't know he'd fought for the freedom of the Spanish people, that for a long time he'd lived underground. I didn't know he was friends with Picasso. I didn't know he was driven around Russia in a black Volga.

If only he had come to see me just once. He would have arrived in our small town in his Volga. Everyone would have seen what kind of car my grandfather had. Maybe Picasso would have sent me a picture—a small picture—through my grandfather. He probably wouldn't have wanted to give me a big one. But a little one? We would have hung that picture in our club, next to the other pictures, under the portraits of the Politburo members. We already had pictures hanging there that the papa of one boy had drawn. The boy's papa was a designer in a factory. The boy was very proud of his papa and his pictures in the club. No, we would have had to hang Picasso's picture in the teachers' room or the director's office. Picasso was cooler than a designer.

My grandfather would have come with the secretary of the district committee of the Communist Party of the Soviet Union. We would have assembled in the club. The director would have delivered a welcome speech and turned the floor over to him. Everyone would have found out that my grandfather was the very best Soviet agent in the world, like Richard Sorge, or Shtirlits. So what if Shtirlits was only in the movies? We were told that the real Shtirlits was still alive and on a secret mission.

Everyone would have seen what kind of grandfather I had. The general secretary of the Communist Party is more important than a teacher, more important than a children's-home director. He would have come out on stage and given a speech on the international situation, and everyone would have realized immediately that he was the most important person there, at home, in Spain. More important than you can imagine. You don't get more important than that. Almost like Leonid Ilich Brezhnev.

He would have seen the top marks in my grade book and my photograph on the school's honor board. He would have loved me, his grandson, immediately. You see, he was a good man, my grandfather. The best grandfather in the world, like grandfather Lenin, like Leonid Ilich Brezhnev. We all knew that Leonid Ilich Brezhnev loved children very much and made sure every day that every Soviet pupil had a happy childhood.

Maybe he didn't have time to come, though. Maybe American spies were following him. Maybe he was part of a conspiracy. He could have written me a letter or even sent a package. I would have received the package, a huge package of chorizo. I wouldn't have eaten the package myself. I would have given everyone a piece of Spanish sausage. The teachers and attendants too. Even our three-legged dog—I would have given her a piece too. Everyone would have eaten my sausage and been amazed. "What unusual sausage they have in Spain, don't you think?" they would have said to each other. Even the dog would have been amazed. But the dog wouldn't have said anything. Dogs don't talk.

Maybe he didn't have money for sausage. Maybe he, like grandfather Lenin, was hiding in a cabin. And maybe, like grandfather Lenin, he didn't eat anything, just drank carrot tea, and when workers and peasants gave him food, he didn't eat it himself but gave away the last crumb to children in children's homes. He could have called. He could have called the director of our children's home on the secret telephone. The director of our children's home was a Communist, and Communists always helped each other. They would have called me into the director's office and told me in strict secrecy about my grandfather, the very best grandfather in the world. I would have understood everything. I was a smart boy. All I needed to know was that he was somewhere and to know that he was on a secret mission and couldn't come. I would have believed he loved me and would come someday. I would have loved him even without the sausage.

Or maybe he wasn't afraid of being found out. Maybe he would have realized that American spies rarely look in on our small provincial town and they would have allowed me to tell everyone about my secret grandfather. Tell them a very little bit. My life would have been completely different from then on. They would have stopped calling me black-assed, and the attendants wouldn't have shouted at me. When the teachers praised me for good marks, it would have been clear to them that I wasn't just the best pupil in the school, but the very best, like my heroic grandfather. I would have been certain that after I finished school they wouldn't take me away to die. My grandfather would come and collect me. Everything would have changed for me. I would have stopped being an orphan. If someone has relatives, he's not an orphan. He's a regular person, like everybody else.

Ignacio didn't come.

Ignacio didn't write.

Ignacio didn't call.

I don't understand him. I'll never understand him.

PSYCHO

The children's home. The right place. If you've ended up in a
children's home, you're lucky. You'll graduate from high
school and go home a changed person, a completely changed
person. You'll have a diploma in your pocket and your whole
life before you. Your whole life before you. Not having feet
or hands is small stuff. Look, your neighbor, Uncle Petya,
came home from the war without legs and it's okay, he's getting along. His wife's a beauty and his daughter is educated,
she's studying foreign languages at the institute. Uncle Petya
did all right for himself: the war taught Uncle Petya life, and
the children's home will teach you.

You'll go home, drink 250 grams apiece with your father,
and light up. Your father will understand everything. He
served in the army and knows what's what in this life. Only
your mama will cry. That's bad. When women cry, it's always
bad. Don't cry, Mama, everything's going to be fine for me,
just like for other people. No worse than for Uncle Petya.

A children's home isn't just a place to board. It's also a
school. A good school. And the teachers are good. There are
smart books and three meals a day. It's a good place, the children's home. Good friends. Real friends. Lifelong friends.

They brought a new kid to the children's home. An ambulant. JCP. Juvenile cerebral palsy. I have juvenile cerebral palsy, too, but everything was more or less okay with the new kid. Just an uneven gait, arms flung out to the sides. His face twitched in a constant attempt to hold back his drool. Smart or dumb—you couldn't tell from his face. The new kid was a puzzle. A new kid was always a puzzle, always a distraction.

The children's home had a funny tradition. When someone with JCP got distracted or lost in thought or was concentrating on something, you were supposed to creep up on him and shout in his ear. He would jerk sharply, and if he didn't keep his wits about him he might fall off his chair. If he just jerked and dropped his pen, it wasn't that funny. The best was to keep an eye on him for when he was drinking hot tea or wine. Wine was the funniest of all. They could always pour him more tea, but not wine. It was his own fault. He'd let his guard down.

I knew that weakness in myself—jerking from a sharp clap or shout. Therefore in an unfamiliar situation I always tried to find an advantageous position, to hide in a corner or crawl under a table. Precaution was standard operating procedure. What's so surprising? It was a children's home.

The new kid walked into the room freely—too freely. He took off his backpack and collapsed on the nearest bed. His feet were facing the door, and his hands were searching his pocket for a handkerchief, as usual. He got it out and wiped away the nonexistent drool.

Suddenly everyone barged in all at once and started laughing. His friends. His future friends.

"Are you the new kid? Why are you lying on my cot?"

"J-just a sec. I'll get up. JCP."

He said "JCP" clearly, with meaning. You could tell he wasn't joking. He was having a hard time and now he'd fallen on the bed.

"Well, get up, don't lie there. Classes are over. Now we're going to scarf down some food. Want some tea?"

They poured him a full cup of tea but took pity on him. So they plopped in a good amount of sugar. You could tell right away they were good guys. That meant they'd accepted him. He summoned up his nerve, sat up, stood carefully, and moved to a chair. He picked the metal mug up, even though it was still hot, and tried to take a sip.

"Paah!" a boy on crutches shouted very loudly—too loudly—in his ear.

He fell. His hand automatically flung the hot mug at his offender. It missed. If it had hit him in the eye! It doesn't hurt to dream. Rarely do you win the lottery. The mug cut the beast's temple. At most he'd have a bruise, no more. A minute. Just a minute. Just a minute while they enjoyed a laugh together.

One, two, three . . .

Remember what you read about Cassius Clay or Muhammad Ali? It doesn't matter. They still don't know. They can't imagine that there, in Chuvashia, you're the city boxing champ among the healthy. "Among the healthy" is a title you've awarded yourself. All the other titles, on the contrary, limit you. "World champ among the healthy" sounds like a personal insult. But you haven't insulted anyone. A referee couldn't find fault with that. If there's drool running from your helmet, it's out of rage. If your arms are trembling and your legs are dancing—that's the trainer's tactics. Always stay in form. In form. Always play healthy. Undercut. In fact, you already know that healthy people aren't always healthy. That only sometimes do they make the effort to go after specific goals. But you're always making the effort. Now it doesn't matter whether you strike with the left or right, because your arms aren't working. But if you have to, if you really have to, you can make the effort, through the pain, the nervous tension, and the revulsion for the extra drooling. Then you can. Then you can do anything. You can do anything and no one can stop you. Then—an accurate blow to your opponent's helmet. A good blow. Like always. Like your whole life. The usual. After all, no one applauds when you button your fly. They button their flies every day, and they don't get a medal for that. The mayor doesn't shake their hand at an official reception.

Four, five, six . . .

You have to get up. Your wet shirt and shoulder, now burned from the boiling water, is nothing. It could be much worse. Anything could happen. They could fall on you at night, cover you with a blanket, and beat you. Just like that. Because you're the new kid. So you know your place. Or rush you en masse, out in the open. That's always better, when it's out in the open. Actually, it isn't even evening. Night is coming and they're going to beat you up. That's why you have to get up. Right now. Be strong and cruel. You don't want to fight, you don't want to at all, but you have to.

He got up. Odd, they were still laughing. They didn't get it. He took a quick look around. He walked over to the boy who'd shouted in his ear. A little boy, a couple of years younger than him, frail, on crutches. What had he done that for? Odd. He hit him, the boy fell down, the crutches flew up. He started beating him. They didn't let him beat him for long. They jumped him from behind and pulled him off.

"What's the matter with you? He was joking. Can't you take a joke?"

"Y-y-yes."

Damn! The stuttering comes at the worst possible moment. Now they think you're scared.

They let him go. He got up again. He slowly stood up and walked toward the boy lying on the floor. You have to beat him. Beat him for a long time. Then they'll believe you're serious. Then they'll treat you like a human being.

"Where are you going? Cut it out. That's enough."

A boy stepped in front of him, apparently healthy, apparently his age. You can't always detect a disability right away, though. When he walked over he seemed to be dragging his foot slightly.

"Cut it out. Cool it. My name's Hamid."

He took aim at Hamid. Okay, first the jaw—and he'd fall. Then he could fall on him and beat him for a long time. Not that they'd let him, of course. They'd intervene. Then he'd have to fight them all at once. Might as well get started.

Hamid understood immediately. He took a step back and smiled.

"What's wrong with you? Are you psycho? Now you're going to beat me? What did I ever do to you? Kolka was joking, just joking, and you hit him. You're even. That's enough."

"Fine. That's enough. Tonight I'll kill him. Or he'll kill me."

Hamid smiled again.

"Have you been reading too many prison books? This isn't a prison. It's a children's home. Just a children's home. No one kills anyone. And they don't fight much. Get it? Kolka was just joking. Why don't you sit down and drink your tea?"

"I've already had enough."

Hamid is wonderful. You can tell immediately he has a head on his shoulders and knows his way around a children's home.

"Want some wine?"

"I've got three rubles."

"You have money too?"

"Should I give you all of it right away?"

"Don't get angry, I was joking."

His lips started to tremble and his head jerked a little to one side.

Hamid understood. He understood everything.

"No need. Don't get so worked up. Your money is your money. No one's going to take it away. They don't steal much either. What's your name?"

"Alexei."

"Lyokha, then?"

"Alexei."

Alexei took a step forward. He was going to have to fight after all.

"Fine. You're Alexei. But can't I call you Lyokha, too? What's the difference? It's not an insult. Let's shake."

They shook hands.

"Bring anything to eat?"

Alexei smiled, took his heavy backpack from the bed, and tossed it on the table. He tugged at the cords and the backpack fell open. He laid out its contents, and from the bottom of the backpack he took out two five-kilo dumbbells. He stepped away and sat down on the bed.

"Have at it!"

Hamid laid the provisions out on the table very deliberately. Lard, onions, garlic, a few cans of meat. No candies, nothing sweet. He pushed a jar of fruit to one side.

"My grandmother gave me the fruit. I didn't want to take it," Lyokha, embarrassed and trying to vindicate himself, was almost stuttering.

"That's fine, you've got good food. And the fruit will come in handy, too. We can use it to cut the vodka. You didn't bring any cigarettes?"

"I don't smoke."

"And rightly so. Neither do I."

That night they drank wine.

They got out their knives and cut bread and lard.

Hamid made neat lard sandwiches and put one on the table in front of himself and one in front of Alexei.

Alexei was about to intervene, as if to say, *I can use a knife myself,* but Hamid didn't even begin to listen.

"Relax. Help's nothing to sneer at. I can cut faster than you, right?"

Hamid got out the bottle and opened it. He poured himself a full glass and slowly drank it down. He poured a second for Lyokha.

"Can you put down a full one?"

"Put it in my mug."

He took an aluminum mug with a big handle out of his backpack.

"This new kid's not so dumb, he's got brains. The glass holds two hundred grams and the mug a whole four hundred."

"You don't get it. I can't lift a glass. Pour half a mug if you want."

"Whatever. I'll pour a full one, and you drink it. You'll skip a turn, that's all."

Alexei took his chair and moved it to the other end of the table, so he'd have his back to the window. He put a dumbbell on the table in front of him. Hamid poured a full mug of wine and put it on the table in front of Alexei.

It's not hard. Drinking from a mug isn't hard at all. You have to grab the handle with your right hand, press the left palm solidly against the mug, and drink slowly. It doesn't matter whether it's tea or wine.

No one said a thing while he was drinking. Not so bad, this new kid. The very first day he drank down a mug of wine without taking a breath. Drank it all and put the mug down on the table. He took his handkerchief out of his pocket, wiped his face, and looked around.

Hamid offered Alexei a sandwich.

"A bite to eat?"

"Later."

"Don't take this wrong, Lyokha, but please get the dumbbell off the table. You're some kind of nut case and you could still give someone a good wallop."

The wine had begun to take effect. Lyokha started laughing. He laughed loudly and merrily. He stowed the dumbbell under the table. He reached for his sandwich and began to eat.

A good children's home, a proper one. And the children were good, too.

FATHER FROST

It's spring. I'm sitting around with a friend. Two upperclassmen in wheelchairs. My friend is smoking. Smoking without bothering to hide the cigarette in his fist or look over his shoulder when a teacher walks by. The teachers ignore him, too. Let him smoke. Let him do what he wants. He has myopathy anyway. A progressive disease. No one knows how long he'll live. My friend's lucky. This spring they're going to take him home. For good.

"You know, Ruben. This year Father Frost wasn't the real thing."

"Are you out of your mind? What Father Frost? How old are you?"

"You don't get it."

He smokes his cigarette down and uses it to light his next. His slender, precise fingers carefully put the butt into a matchbox. Slow, precise movements. I wouldn't be able to do that.

"You don't understand, Ruben. New Year's was when I first got really sick—that was before I started school. I still didn't know what was wrong with me. My parents called in Father Frost. He came late that night. I wasn't asleep and they'd promised me Father Frost. Mama looked and saw I wasn't sleeping so she turned on the lights on the tree. Papa invited him into the kitchen but instead he came straight in to see me. He saw the medicine on my night table and the crutches. He said to Papa: 'What would we do in the kitchen? Let's go drink under your tree. My shift's over anyway.' They brought in the table, vodka, and snacks from the kitchen. It was great. And they didn't make me recite poetry. They poured me a glass of lemonade. They each tossed back their first and Father Frost took off his beard. A great Father Frost, we called him Uncle Petya. There just aren't any sober Father Frosts."

I knew what he meant. And I thought about my own Father Frosts. Old and young, male and female. The Father Frost who was our lady literature teacher, and the young Father Frosts who were students at the teachers' institute. The Father Frosts who were doctors—very often they were doctors.

Once in my life I saw a real Father Frost. He came in merry and drunk. Father Frost complete with a red nose. He said, "Hello, children," in a ringing bass voice. We answered the way we were supposed to: "Hello, Father Frost." Father Frost danced and sang. He recited poems. He looked at us easily and attentively. He didn't avert his eyes from the tots in the carnival costumes. When they turned on the slow music, he danced with an armless girl from the upper classes.

We reminisce. We reminisce about how the year before a very young Father Frost read the children's names off a sheet of paper, got mixed up, turned red, and stammered, and when the time came to pass out the presents, all of a sudden he didn't feel so good. They took him into the teachers' room and gave him valerian drops.

This other Father Frost was what was wanted. He left his magic wand at the door when he came in. He put the hokey sack of presents in front of the tots. The little boys didn't take anything out of the bag—they were too shy. Then he spilled all the candies on the floor right under the tree.

Toward the end of our holiday party, Father Frost went backstage. He returned without his beard and coat, wearing his dress uniform. He put on his glasses and took a piece of paper out of his pocket that had been folded in fourths. He read—he had a slight stutter—something about the Party and the government, about the ultimate victory of communism, about our happy childhood. Then, putting the correct paper back in his pocket, he made a loud announcement: "And now, my Snowmaidens will pass out presents to everyone!" He waited for the clapping to die down and walked off the stage and over to the small table where our children's-home director was sitting. Young fellows with cadets' epaulets who didn't look anything like Snowmaidens carried big cardboard boxes of presents into the auditorium. They passed out all the presents very quickly and properly. To everyone—children and grown-ups alike. It was a good New Year's, the best New Year's of my life.

My friend is smoking. I've been telling him about my own real Father Frost. We understand each other.

"You're right," he says. "There is no such thing as a sober Father Frost. Sober Father Frosts aren't the real thing."

THE DOG

She came all by herself. She turned in at the gate, struggled up on the bench, and lay there, wagging her tail. It was evening. Night, almost. An older boy who'd gone out into the yard for a smoke saw the dog. He was a grown man already, an upperclassman. He put away the cigarette and quickly brought some water in a can.

Without words, invisibly, the news spread: "a dog." The usual routine flew out the window and the children dashed outside, crowding around the bench. Each one wanted to pet and admire the dog.

Keeping dogs at a children's home was against health regulations. Dogs spread infection and dogs can have worms. From time to time, some mutt would wander in and go over to the dining room. The children would sneak food to it and the grown-ups would drive it away with sticks. That was all okay, all as it should be. In the morning the dog would be gone. At night a truck would have come and taken the dog away. We were told they made soap from dogs. In the morning the girls would come to school with tear-stained eyes. The boys didn't cry. Boys weren't supposed to cry. The upperclassmen would smoke, though, hardly hiding it. They would smoke right in front of the teachers, just asking for trouble. The grown-ups tried not to react. The grown-ups were sure the children just needed time, that the children would forget everything. Smart grown-ups.

Nearly everyone went outside. We stood or sat in silence.

An elderly nurse emerged from the clinic. She walked up and took a quick look at the dog.

"Take the dog away. The children need to wash their hands with soap and go to bed. Immediately. What's going on here?"

A boy on crutches, a preschooler. A gypsy. He scrambled onto the bench and stood in front of the woman.

"You can't take her away. She's good. She came to see us all by herself."

The nurse looked at the child with disdain. She'd been around the block. She was used to this. She knew better. She knew exactly what these children needed.

"Go to bed, son. Who's the duty boy? Who's responsible for lights-out?"

There wasn't any duty boy. The duty boy had gone to the toilet as a precaution and was sitting there, smoking and waiting.

The gypsy stood there, confidently, hands on his crutches, his foot on the ground. He wasn't afraid of grown-ups. He had the children's home behind him, the entire children's home. Right now, he had everyone behind him.

"You can't take her away. She's missing a foot!"

The nurse knelt in front of the boy.

"Don't say 'foot,' say 'paw.' Understand? Dogs have paws, and people have feet."

She stopped short. She jerked her head back, stood up,

and straightened her coat. Her face was calm and intense. Not a shadow of doubt. The face of a woman who was no longer young but was certain she was right.

She went away and returned quickly. She opened her bag of instruments.

"Hold her."

The older boys held the dog down, and the nurse cut the dirty clumps of fur from her sides. She poured iodine on the open wounds. The dog shuddered, the boys held on to her, and the nurse did her job calmly and deftly. Toward the end she used her sharp scissors to cut off a flap of skin on the dog's paw. She bandaged it up.

"Burn the fur. Tomorrow we'll call in the veterinarian and give her all her shots. You have to change the dressing on her paw every day. I'll give you the bandages. If I see anything amiss—the dog will be gone. Do I make myself clear?"

She put away her instruments and went to the clinic. She gave a very young aide a stern look.

"Everyone needs to wash their hands immediately and go to bed. Lights out."

If it was lights-out it was lights-out. Everyone scattered. Only the gypsy boy stayed with the dog. He was petting her on the head and didn't want to leave. The dog was wagging her tail sluggishly and looking placidly at the pieces of smoked sausage in front of her.

An aide came into the yard and sat down beside them on the bench.

"Go to bed. It's late."

The boy didn't say a word.

She was a young aide, just out of school. What kind of teacher could she ever be? She slid a little closer and reached out to stroke the boy's head, but he edged away, so she petted the dog.

"Go on, go to bed. Your dog has nowhere to go. I called the director and he said he'd be watching your behavior and would decide what to do with the dog. They won't take the dog away. Not today, anyway."

The dog quietly ate her fill. Each one of us wanted to feed the dog. The tots hid pieces of bread from breakfast in their pockets for her. The girls brought her the blini they made in cooking class. The sullen, hard-nosed boys from the upper classes brought her snacks left over from their drinking parties. The cook—secretly at first, then openly—fed her kitchen scraps.

Over the winter, the dog grew a luxurious rust-colored coat. That's what we called her—Rusty. The girls would brush her twenty times a day and braid her fur. She put up with all of it. She liked the girls better than the boys.

The boys played with her. The boys read books on animal training. The dog jumped through a hoop and shook her right, then left forepaw. She knew commands: "stay," "sit," "lie down." Her favorite command was "fetch." She could chase a ball for hours. She would put the ball right in the hands of those in wheelchairs. She played with everyone and went to everyone. If someone couldn't throw a ball, she would just rest her head in his lap. She was a smart dog. She understood everything and could do everything. She just couldn't walk on her one hind leg. Not that she had to do a dance for a piece of bread, or beg or curry favor with people. They gave her food anyway.

One day on his way in to work, the children's-home director, a stern man with a black briefcase, leaned over the dog and ruffled her rusty fur. He asked her gravely, "How's life treating you? No complaints? Are your papers in order?"

Her veterinary papers were in perfect order. Everything about her was in order. She raced around on three legs and yelped cheerfully at strangers. She recognized us instantly, even those who weren't enrolled in the school yet and those who hadn't been at our home for very long. She distinguished us from strangers unerringly.

Sometimes stray dogs would pay us a visit. Now it wasn't just the grown-ups who drove stray dogs away with sticks. Stray dogs were banned from the restricted territory of the home. Stray dogs had worms and fleas. We fired our sling-shots at stray dogs. In the spring a man came. He said he was her former owner. We didn't believe him. He came in and reached out to pet Rusty. We believed him. That good dog hurled herself to the ground and started growling. Her menacing growl swelled to a howl. She pressed her belly to the ground and let up a howl. She jumped up, stuck her tail between her legs, and ran off to the furnace room.

The first morning of her life in the home, the children had built a little house for her in shop class. They had a special design for the doghouse. Double walls and a warm wooden floor. The girls lined the house with old blankets. Someone brought a pillow. A pillow from home that didn't have the institution's stamp. The little boys carried cozy, homey things to the house, their favorite toys. The older girls regularly handed all this back to the boys and chastised them, explaining that they shouldn't do that—it was pointless. From time to time someone would bring cozy human presents to the doghouse anyway. She slept in that doghouse. She liked it. In the winter, when it was especially cold, the dog slept in the furnace room. Our very good-hearted stoker had once been a student in our home. He had arms and legs. He was a healthy, handsome muzhik. Just not very bright. And almost mute. In ten years of schooling he never did learn how to read or write. Who on earth needed him in that cold world of strangers outside our gate? When he was sad, he bought vodka. Vodka and ice cream. He drank the vodka himself and shared the ice cream with the dog. Often he sat there drunk next to the furnace rambling on about something very important while the dog ate ice-cream bar after ice-cream bar. It felt good to be together. No one yelled at him for the vodka. Everybody knew that no matter how much he drank, the furnace wouldn't go out. Even incredibly drunk, he conscientiously shoveled coal into the furnace. A fine stoker.

The stranger was waving his arms about, arguing and making demands. The grown-ups ignored his arguments. The grown-ups threatened to call the police. He left and stood outside the gate, waiting for something.

The black-eyed boy with the shaven head, the sharp little gypsy. He hopped along quickly on his crutches, wearing holes in the sole of his one boot. He came up, examined the stranger carefully, and tugged at his sleeve.

"Hey, buy my little knife."

He shook a penknife with a shiny composite handle out of his sleeve and into his hand. He threw his arm back—and the knife was gone. Lowered it—and the knife lay once again on his outstretched palm. Simple sleight of hand.

The man leaned toward the boy.

"Give it here. You're too young to be fooling around with toys like that."

"Okay. Give me the money. It's my knife."

The boy threw the knife over his shoulder and showed him empty hands. He picked up his crutches and was all set to run away.

"Wait up. Call one of the older boys over."

An upperclassman came out. He was graduating this year. A tall boy with reddish bangs that fell right into his eyes and hair that covered his ears. His sleeve was neatly tucked into his belt.

They sat down on the bench by the gate. The boy took his cigarettes from his pocket, tapped a cigarette out of the pack, and grabbed it with his lips. Then he put the pack back in his pocket. He got out a matchbox. Steadying the box in his palm with his pinky, he deftly removed a match from the box with his thumb and index finger, struck it, and lit up. It all happened fast, very fast.

"So what's on your mind?"

"Give me back my dog. I can see, I'm not a little kid. She's had a good feed with you and her fur's grown in. I'll give you a bottle of vodka."

The boy smoked in silence.

"Oh, all right, I'm not greedy. I'll give you two. Two bottles of vodka."

"It's your dog?"

"Yes."

"Let's check that out. Was she born without her foot or did she get that way? Watch out, I'm going to figure this out."

"She got that way."

"So what do you need her so badly for all of a sudden?"

"I'm going to make a hat. You've fed her so well. She'll make a good hat."

"I see. All right then, bring the vodka and take the dog away."

"What do you mean, 'take the dog away'? You bring her out to me on the leash."

"Do you have the leash with you?"

"Of course."

The boy finished smoking and looked the man up and down. He was short, a head shorter than the boy.

"Hey, listen, why don't you buy my knife?"

"Is everyone here crazy? One of you already offered me his. Some snot-nosed kid."

"You're right, he is a snot-nosed kid, and his knife's crap. You should buy mine."

The boy lifted the hand with the knife to the man's face and pressed a button. The blade whipped out—a long, slender blade. With an almost imperceptible movement of his expert hand he folded the knife back up. And pushed the button again. He folded the knife up again and put it back in his pocket.

"Or maybe you need brass knuckles. Come to the gate as soon as it gets dark. Don't be shy. I make good brass knuckles. I won't charge you a lot."

"I need the dog."

"If you say so."

He stood up and went to the gate. He stopped for a minute, smiled, and suddenly beamed with joy. As if he had remembered something near and dear to his heart.

"Hey, listen, let's go right now and you take her away. For free."

The man cheered up.

"Let's go."

"Only you'd better watch out. She's in the furnace room right now and the stoker's been drinking. He probably brought in a case of vodka yesterday. Our stoker's a pretty sturdy muzhik. He can lift a car by its bumper with one hand—doesn't need a jack. He's not quite right in the head, though. He doesn't hear so well. Just speak slowly and he'll understand. And you know what? You should start with the main point, the hat. He'll understand about the hat."

The man finally figured out that they were playing with him. He swore under his breath and slunk off. These children's-home kids were savages, and mean.

One day. One day I'll buy myself a dog. A smart Labrador, purebred, an expensive beast. He'll open doors for me and give me things I've dropped. Someday I'll forget this children's-home dog. A fine dog, rusty, missing a paw.

HANDS

I don't have hands. What I'm forced to make do with can only be called hands at a stretch. I'm used to it. I can type on the computer with my left index finger and I can hold a spoon in my right hand and eat tolerably well.

You can live without hands. I knew a guy without hands who had adapted pretty well to his situation. He did everything with his feet. He ate with his feet, combed his hair with his feet, and got dressed and undressed with his feet. He shaved with his feet. He even learned to sew on buttons. He could thread a needle himself, too. Every day he trained his little-boy body. He worked out. In fights at the home he could strike his opponent in the kisser or jaw with his foot without hardly trying. A normal children's-home guy.

Living without hands isn't that hard if you have all the rest. All the rest—my body—developed even worse than my hands. My hands are the main thing. You might say that the main thing about a person is his head. Or you might not. Obviously a head can't survive without hands. It doesn't matter whether the hands are yours or someone else's.

Sergey had hands. Two strong, perfectly healthy hands.

Above the waist he was totally fine. Hands, shoulders, head. A blond head. Sergey Mikhailov. Seryozha.

In school he was one of the best pupils. That wasn't enough for him. He was constantly reading science fiction magazines, mailing entries in to contests for schoolchildren, completing assignments for magazines and submitting them, so they would send him various certificates.

Below the waist his two twisted legs rested in a permanent lotus position. Below the waist he had no feeling, absolutely none, which meant he always had to carry around a bedpan. When the urine spilled over the bedpan, he changed his pants himself. He did everything himself. He didn't have to call for the attendants, to demean himself, to ask for help. He himself could help others, the ones who were even less fortunate. He fed one of his friends with a spoon, he helped him wash his hair and change his clothes.

He didn't have parents. He wasn't an ambulant. When he finished school they took him away to an old folks' home.

In the old folks' home they put him in a ward with two old men. Harmless old men. One, a shoemaker, would heat shoemaker's glue on a hot plate; the other, a goner, was completely out of it, and urine dripped from his bed. They wouldn't give Seryozha a change of sheets. They explained to him that he was supposed to change his pants once every ten days.

He lay in the ward for three weeks with the smell of shit and shoemaker's glue. For three weeks he refused to eat and tried to drink as little water as possible. Hooked up to his urinal, he couldn't force himself to crawl outside naked to see the sun one last time. Three weeks later he was dead.

In a year they were supposed to take me to that old folks' home. Sergey had arms, and I didn't.

THE OLD FOLKS' HOME

I'd been afraid of ending up in a loony bin or an old folks' home since I was ten.

It was easy not to end up in a loony bin. You just had to behave well, obey your elders, and not complain. Never complain. Those who complained about the bad food or objected to what the grown-ups did were periodically carted off to the loony bin. They would come back very quiet and obedient, but at night they would tell us terrible stories about the evil orderlies.

Everyone who couldn't walk ended up in an old folks' home. Not for any particular reason, just because. The only ones who escaped this fate were the ones who could acquire a trade. After graduation, the smart students went to institutes, and those who weren't so bright went to technical or vocational schools. Only the most assiduous and gifted pupils went to institutes. I was a better student than anyone. But I wasn't ambulant.

Sometimes after graduation an ambulant was taken home by his relatives. I didn't have any relatives.

Everything changed for me after I found out that one fine day they would take me to that awful place, put me on a bed, and leave me to die without food or care. The teachers and aides lost their authority and wisdom in my eyes. Very often as I listened to a teacher I would find myself thinking that this might be the very person who would send me away to die.

They would tell me about theorems and inequalities, and I would automatically absorb the lesson's material.

They would tell me about great writers, but I was not interested.

They would tell me about the Fascist concentration camps, and I would burst into tears.

When yet another attendant started yelling at me yet again, I would think with gratitude that she was right, she had a right to shout at me, because she was taking care of me. There, where they were going to take me, no one would bring me a bedpan. She, this semiliterate woman, was good, and I was bad. Bad because I called for the attendants too often and because I ate too much. Bad because I had been given birth to by a black-assed bitch who abandoned me to these fine, good people. I was bad. To become good took very little, just the tiniest thing. Something almost anyone, even the stupidest person, could do. I just had to stand up and walk.

The teachers didn't understand why I cried all the time. Why I didn't want to talk to any of them or write compositions on a topic of my own choosing. Even the smartest and best of them, the very, very best, refused to talk to me about my future. Other topics didn't interest me.

That year, when I finished my eight years of schooling, they shut down the ninth- and tenth-year classes. The upperclassmen were dispersed to other children's homes, and some were taken off to the loony bin. Children perfectly fine in the head were taken to a common loony bin. They were unlucky. As often happens with people who have cerebral palsy, they had speech defects. The commission that came did not stand on ceremony, but shipped them off to a special boarding school for the mentally retarded.

I stayed on as the sole overage child. According to law, I had the right to ten years of schooling, but no one cared about the law.

They took me to an old folks' home.

The children's-home bus shook horribly as it rode over the bumps. The children's-home director himself was taking me to the old folks' home. His broad smile revealed his gold teeth, and he was smoking Kosmos cigarettes, which were all he ever smoked. He was smoking and looking straight ahead through the window.

They lifted me out of the bus in my wheelchair. I was, after all, a privileged invalid. Children's-home graduates weren't supposed to keep their wheelchairs. They were taken away to old folks' homes without their wheelchairs, put in a bed, and left to rot. According to law, the old folks' home was supposed to issue replacement wheelchairs within a year, but that was according to law. In the old folks' home where they took me there was just one wheelchair. For everyone. Those who could crawl to it from their bed independently took turns taking rides in it. The rides were restricted to the home's porch.

It was autumn. September. Not yet cold. A low-slung wooden structure built before the Revolution. No fence. Odd people wearing homespun coats and caps with earflaps were wandering around a yard overgrown with burdock.

A chorus was singing. The omnipresent chorus of elderly

female voices. You couldn't see the old women; they were all inside. You could hear the singing coming from there:

Oh, the guelder blossoms
In the meadow by the brook.
A fellow young and handsome
I loved when first I looked . . .

Never. Never before or after have I heard that kind of fatalistic, plaintive singing. When I was riding in the bus I'd been worried. After I heard the chorus, my worry subsided into apathy. I didn't care.

They pushed my wheelchair inside. The hallway was dark and smelled of damp and mice. They steered me into a room, walked out, and left me there.

A small room. Bare walls. Two iron cots and a wooden table.

After a while the children's-home director walked into the room with an official from the old folks' home and an attendant. I could tell she was an attendant by her blue coat.

The attendant walked up to me. She examined me closely.

"But he's such a young, little fellow! What's going on? To think they're bringing us ones like this now. What's going on? People have no more conscience."

She walked out.

The director was smoking nervously and briskly continuing his interrupted conversation.

"Won't you take him? It's really essential."

"Don't ask. You must understand. He's sixteen now. Right?"

"Fifteen," I corrected him mechanically.

"Fifteen," the man conceded. "He's going to die here in a month, two maximum. I only have the right to bury people who are at least eighteen. This is an old folks' home, understand?

Where am I going to keep him for two years? All the refrigerators are broken. Broken, understand? And remember, do you remember what you told me a year ago when I asked you for help with the refrigerators? Do you? So don't ask. Take him to a home for the mentally retarded. They have the right to bury infants if necessary."

"Don't decide right away, we'll talk. I need to make a call."

They went away.

I sat there alone. It was twilight. A cat ran down the hall.

Suddenly the room was filled with a strange, disgusting smell. It stank more and more. I couldn't figure out what was happening.

The attendant was carrying in a tray. She put the tray on the table and turned on the light. I had the honor of seeing the source of the strange smell. It was mashed peas. A green, sticky mass that looked as awful as it smelled. In addition to the peas, there was a plate of borscht and a piece of bread on the tray. No spoon.

The attendant looked at the tray and noticed the spoon was missing. She went out. She brought back a spoon. The spoon was covered with dried peas. The attendant broke off a crust of my bread and carelessly wiped the spoon with it, then tossed the spoon into the borscht.

She walked over to me. She stared hard.

"No. He won't last the winter. That's for certain."

"Excuse me," I said. "Why is it so dark in here and why is there a draft from the window?"

"This is an isolation room, a good room, and it's close to the stove. But they'll assign you to the general ward for non-ambulants. It's really drafty there. I told you, you won't last the winter. It's an old building."

"Do you have a lot of cats?"

"No, we don't have any cats."

"But I saw a cat run down the hall."

"That's not a cat, it's a rat."

"What do you mean, a rat? In the daytime?"

"What of it? Day and night. By day it's not so bad, but at night, when they run down the hallway, we lock ourselves in our rooms and we're scared to go out. And they're nasty. A little while ago they ate the ears off a bedridden old lady. Eat now, or it'll get cold."

She walked out.

I brought the plate closer and ate the borscht mechanically. It was shit. The borscht was shit. The peas were shit. Life was shit.

I sat. I thought. Suddenly the director ran into the room. He was rubbing his hands with glee.

"Well now, Gallego, we don't have to leave you here after all. Let's go back, to the children's home. Do you want to go to the children's home?"

"Yes."

"And rightly so, too."

He looked at the plate of food.

"You'll make it back by suppertime. And we won't be taking you to the psychoneurological home either. Understand?" And he slowly repeated: "Ga-lle-go."

"Gonzalez Gallego," I corrected him.

"What's that? You understand a lot. I said Gallego, so it's Gallego."

We arrived at the home. We made it in time for supper.

"Come on, tell us, what's it like there?" a boy in a wheelchair asked me at supper.

"Tonight," I said. "I'll tell you tonight."

LANGUAGE

A home. An old folks' home. My final asylum and refuge. The end. A dead end. I copy irregular English verbs into a notebook. They're carrying a corpse down the hall on a stretcher. The old men and women are discussing tomorrow's menu. I'm copying irregular English verbs into a notebook. The other invalids my age have organized a Young Communists meeting. The home's director gave a welcoming speech in the auditorium dedicated to this latest anniversary of the Great October Socialist Revolution. I'm copying irregular English verbs into a notebook. One old guy, a former prisoner, cracked his crutch over his ward mate's head during his latest drinking spree. One old woman, an honored veteran of labor, hung herself in a closet. A woman in a wheelchair swallowed a handful of sleeping pills so that she could leave this regular world forever. I'm copying irregular English verbs into a notebook.

It's all perfectly regular. I'm not a human being. I haven't earned anything more than this. I didn't become a tractor driver or a scholar. They feed me out of pity. It's all perfectly regular. The way it should be. Regular, regular, regular.

Only the verbs are irregular. They lie down stubbornly in

the notebook after they've edged through the rustle of static on the radio. I'm listening to irregular verbs of the irregular, English, language. They're being dictated by an irregular reader from irregular America. An irregular person in a perfectly regular world, I'm persevering in my study of the English language. I'm studying it for no real reason, to keep from going crazy, to keep from becoming regular.

THE CANE

The old folks' home. A terrible place. People shriveled by impotence and despair, their souls encased in an impervious shell. Nothing surprises anyone. The usual life of the usual poorhouse.

Four attendants were pushing a linen cart. An old man was sitting in the cart and wailing to break your heart. He was wrong. It was his own fault. The night before he had broken his leg, and the head nurse had ordered him moved to the third floor. For someone with a broken leg, the third floor was a death sentence.

His drinking buddies and the other people he knew were on the second floor. On the second floor they passed out meals regularly, and the attendants emptied the bedpans. Ambulant friends could ask a doctor or attendant to bring cookies from the store. On the second floor you were guaranteed to survive if you had healthy hands. You could hold on until your leg healed, until you were ambulant again and they kept you on the list of the living.

The old guy was shouting ominously about his past service at the front and explaining about his forty years' seniority in the mines. He was sternly threatening to complain to a higher authority. His trembling hands held out a handful of orders and medals to the attendants. What a nut! Who cared about his trinkets?

The cart rolled steadily toward the elevator. The attendants weren't listening to him, they were doing their job. The old man's cry got softer and his threats ceased. Clutching desperately to his useless life, he was pleading now, begging them not to move him to the third floor today but to wait a couple of days: "My leg's going to heal up fast and I'll be able to walk." The former miner attempted to move the attendants to pity, but in vain. Then he started to cry. For a moment, for just a moment, he remembered being a human being. In one convulsive movement he grabbed the elevator door in a death grip. But what good are an old man's hands against the strength of four healthy women? And so, weeping and moaning, he was rolled into the elevator. That was it. Once there had been a human being—and now there wasn't.

Residents came to our institution by various routes. Some were brought by relatives; some came of their own accord, weary of struggling with the burdens of life at liberty. The most confident, most unambivalent feelings toward the poorhouse were those held by the ex-cons. Ex-cons, tough old wolves who had acquired neither home nor family on the outside, would come straight to us after serving out their prison term.

There had been a commotion and shouting since morning. The attendants had been swearing at a lively but withered old man. In vain. He hadn't intended to add to their workload.

It was the same old story. One minute, he'd been playing cards and drinking vodka with his ward mate. Either his card hadn't followed suit or his neighbor had tried to cheat—who's to say?—but the old man took his cane and whacked his drinking buddy on the head hard enough to splatter blood all over the room and then the toilet, where they had dragged the crippled card player, and then the hall from the ward to the toilet. He hadn't meant to soil the floor, he hadn't, but that's what had happened.

As soon as the old guy had arrived at the home he'd filled his ordinary aluminum cane with pig iron and steadied himself with it when he walked. A thirty-year prison term had taught him to watch his back. And a good heavy cane isn't bad to have in a fight. He liked his weapon, and he liked having at hand an absolute guarantee of his personal inviolability. But he was sincerely apologetic about the soiled floor. They forgave him, but to keep him from temptation they moved him to a separate room.

As usual, the attendants had raised a fuss a little earlier that morning. Nothing too terrible. The ex-prisoner had had a stroke. A stroke was serious business. When the old man woke up, the right side of his body wouldn't obey his damaged brain. His right arm hung like a noose, and his heavy right leg wouldn't stir. A half-faced smile and a terrible sentence: the third floor. The fussy head nurse was running around giving orders. After they finished their breakfast, the attendants went off cheerfully, in no particular rush, to do their boss's bidding. There was no point rushing; that old man wasn't going anywhere.

But the old prisoner was in no rush to reach the next world. He wasn't tired of the nice sun, and he hadn't drunk his full allotment of vodka. Groaning heavily, he picked the cane up with his left hand and lay there in wait.

The attendants arrived. They looked in amazement at the old man with the raised cane.

Before they could collect themselves, the old prisoner took one look at them and started talking. He had the heavy, prickly gaze of a cornered beast. The heavy cane did not shake in his hand.

"What? Come to take me, you bitches? Come on, get close. Are you going to be first? Or you? I'll crack your head open, I promise. I won't kill you, but I'll cripple you."

He looked at them confidently, directly. The muzhik understood he was all flash. What could he, a paralyzed man, do against four healthy country women? They could have fallen on him at once and taken the stick away. Only no one wanted to be first. They were afraid of injuries, they were afraid of his stick. After all, the ex-con would strike without regret.

Without a moment's hesitation, the women exited. The head nurse ran up and down the hallway shouting at them, trying to coax them into it—in vain. They advised her to go in and take away the old prisoner's stick first.

In a helpless rage, the head nurse called the guard.

The policeman on duty, a serious muzhik a couple of years shy of his pension, arrived at her urgent summons. Military bearing, a pistol in his holster.

He walked into the ex-con's room and took a look at the disturber of the peace. On the bed lay a withered old man holding a cane in his hand for some reason.

"Are you disturbing the peace?"

"What do you mean, citizen officer, what peace? Don't you see how bent I am?"

The policeman leaned over the sick man and threw back the sheet.

"Did they call the doctor?"

"The nurse came and gave me a shot."

"What do they need from me, then?"

"You get the stick away from him and we can take it from there," the head nurse broke into the conversation.

"Get out, citizen, and don't interfere. I'm conducting an investigation," the policeman shut her up. He closed the door, moved the chair closer to the bed, and sat down.

"The cops in the slammer weren't as fierce as they are here," the ex-con tried to justify himself. "They want to move me to the third floor. That's where they have the goners' unit."

"What for?"

"Who knows? Women . . ."

"Women . . ." the policeman repeated thoughtfully. "I don't understand them."

For a while they didn't say anything.

The policeman stood up and went out.

"All right, citizens. I've had an instructive chat with your patient. He promised to be better and not to disturb the peace anymore. If he does do something serious, have no doubt: we'll come, write up the papers, and prosecute him to the full extent of the law."

He straightened his cap, gave the women in white coats a stern look, and walked toward the exit.

The old man did hold on after his stroke. Whether the head nurse's angina shots had helped, or his ferocious thirst for life had pulled him back from the next world, little by little he began sitting up, and finally he got back on his feet. He would walk all over the home dragging his paralyzed leg, confidently holding his cane in his left hand. A good heavy cane. An excellent thing. And reliable.

SINNER

The old folks' home. Day flows into night, and night flows seamlessly into day. Seasons run together and time recedes. Nothing happens and nothing surprises. The same faces, the same conversations. Only once in a while does familiar reality stir, rebel, and spit out something completely unusual that doesn't mesh with simple, ordinary concepts.

She had lived at the home always, since the day it opened, it seemed. Modest and quiet, she was a little person in a big, cruel world. A little woman. No taller than a five-year-old child, her dear little arms and legs so loosely attached at her frail joints that she couldn't walk. Lying face down on a trolley, she pushed herself along and that was how she got around.

This woman worked in the funeral services workshop. We had a shop like that in our house of sorrow. The old ladies fashioned coffin decorations, wreaths made of artificial flowers and other such trumpery, for nearly all the deceased of that small town. Wreaths could be ordered at the workshop next to the cemetery as well, but it was generally believed that the wreaths there were more expensive and made any old way, without the proper respect for such sensitive and significant objects. Year after year she twisted colored paper into neat little flowers, which she wove into cemetery wreaths, a respectful expression of touching concern for the dead.

No one ever insulted this unfortunate woman. The employees never paid any attention to her trolley as it went slowly down the hall. She didn't ask for help, and got to the toilet and cafeteria by herself. The rowdy drunks who from time to time terrorized all the poorhouse inhabitants would never have laid a finger on the defenseless creature.

And so she lived. During the day she twisted flowers for the deceased, and in the evening she tatted napkins or embroidered linens. Day after day, year after year. She lived just fine. Gradually she had adapted her small room to her own modest measurements. A mattress on the floor, a low table, a doll's chair, lace towels and embroidered cushions.

She had lived a long time, too long. The woman was well past forty. She'd overstayed her welcome. At one of their meetings, the management decided that it was time to transfer her to the third floor. According to the usual plan. The normal workings of a well-oiled machine. And on the third floor they would put her on an ordinary big bed in a room with three goners and leave her to a slow death. They'd deprive her of her one luxury: the freedom to take care of herself.

She'd lived her whole long life quietly and had never asked the management for anything, but now, suddenly, she signed up to see the director. She sat in line for hours waiting for her legitimate right to see him, and then begged him not to evict her from her little room, pleaded to be allowed to live out her days in familiar surroundings. He listened to her without a change of expression and refused her without a

change of expression, then banished her from the waiting line.

The night before the scheduled move she hung herself on her door handle. Sinner.

THE OFFICER

They brought a new guy to the old folks' home. A big man
without legs, he sat on a low trolley. His gaze swept the area
confidently as he rolled slowly into the building. He oriented
himself immediately, without any help. He rolled around our
entire three-story building, taking his time, section by section. He started with the cafeteria. It was dinnertime. He
looked to see what they were serving, gave a grim chuckle,
but didn't eat. He took the elevator to the third floor—the
mortality floor, the goners' section. Without panic or fuss he
looked into each room and didn't hold his nose or turn away
from the truth. He saw the helpless old men lying motionless
on their beds and heard their moans and cries. Before night-
fall, he returned to the room he'd been assigned to and lay
down on the bed.

It was a fine room on the second floor. With one roommate. On the door was a handsome plaque with the inscrip-
tion: HERE LIVES A VETERAN OF THE GREAT PATRIOTIC WAR.
Decent living conditions. You could go to the cafeteria three
times a day, eat what they were serving, and in the evening
watch television with everyone. An appropriate portion of
his pension would pay, with interest, for the obvious needs of

an elderly man—cigarettes, tea, and cookies. No one and nothing could keep him from buying vodka if he wanted to, or from drinking it with a neighbor, reminiscing about the past, as they told each other what kind of men they'd been, how they'd fought in the war and won. They always won. As long as he had the strength in his hands, he could push his trolley to the toilet and hold a spoon, and as long as he had life he could fight daily for the right to consider himself a human being.

That evening they didn't have any vodka. His roommate was good-hearted. All evening and half the night this quiet old man, who had made peace with this barracks life, listened to the new man's story. In the precise voice of a commander, the legless man described his entire life in detail. No matter how his story began, though, it always boiled down to one thing: in the war he had been a deep-reconnaissance officer.

Deep-reconnaissance officers. Brave, tested fighters, the best of the best, tops. The elite. They picked their way through minefields into enemy territory and went deep into the rear. Not all returned, but those who did went into the enemy's rear over and over. War is war. They never ran away from death, they accepted their missions, they did what they were told. Death wasn't the worst thing that could happen to a man. They feared captivity—the disgrace, the humiliation, the helplessness. There were no prisoners or wounded in deep reconnaissance. According to regulations, anyone who was slowing the group's progress was supposed to shoot himself. A correct instruction. The death of one is better than the death of all. That one killed himself and the others went on—to complete their assignment and strike at the enemy. To take revenge for their country, for their dead friends, for the fact that they had voluntarily taken leave of this life for the sake of the common cause. If an injury was so serious that the soldier couldn't shoot himself, there was always a friend by his side who was compelled to help. A real friend, not a blowhard, not some drinking buddy or someone who happened to live in your apartment building. Someone who wouldn't betray you, who would share his last crust of bread and his next-to-last bullet.

The officer went on and on with his story. About how he'd stepped on a mine. How he'd pleaded with his friend: "Shoot me." The accident had happened close to the border, so his friend carried him back to their own territory, ten kilometers or so—not the deep rear. How his whole life he'd feared being a burden, how he'd worked in a cooperative and sewn stuffed animals. He'd married and raised children. He had good children, only now they didn't need a legless old man.

Before dawn, the officer sawed his throat open with a penknife. He sawed for a long time. A small, dull little knife. And his poor roommate heard nothing, though he was an old man and slept lightly. Not a sound, not a moan.

The deep-reconnaissance officer died. He died correctly, by the book. Only he hadn't had a friend, a real friend nearby to smoke one last cigarette with him, to hand him a pistol and step aside tactfully, so as not to interfere. No, he hadn't had a friend by his side. What a pity.

THE FEEDER

The old women liked to die in the spring. People died in all seasons, in a steady trickle, but most of all they died in the spring. In the spring it got warmer in the wards, in the spring they opened the doors and windows, letting fresh air into the stuffy world of the old folks' home. Life got better in the spring. All winter the old women clung stubbornly to life, waiting for spring so they could let go and surrender to the will of nature and die in peace. There were far fewer old men in the home. The old men died without regard for seasonal changes. If life refused to tempt them with a bottle of vodka or a tasty snack, they went to the next world without a fight.

I'm sitting in the yard at the home. I'm sitting alone. I'm not bored. I'm not bored at all. I'm looking at spring. I'm young, and I'm certain I'll live many years more in this world. For me, spring doesn't mean what it does for the old folks.

Someone appears in the doorway. A decrepit old woman is walking, pushing a chair in front of her. Violently she jerks her entire body straight and balances for a moment on her legs while her hands move the chair a few centimeters forward. Then, leaning heavily on the back of the chair, she slowly drags her feet toward it. After taking a look around and failing to spot any familiar faces in the yard, she moves confidently in my direction. One more companion, one more story.

The old woman comes up to me, stops her chair in front of my wheelchair, and sits down slowly and heavily.

All through the war she had worked on a collective farm. Worked from morning till night. They weren't paid money. What money? They had one objective: everything for the front; everything for victory. On workdays they were issued groats. They made hot cereal out of the groats. Cereal, nothing more. Not even bread. After the war things got a little easier, because her husband came home alive and unharmed. She and her husband applied to go to the city. Her husband became a driver and she went to work in a sewing factory. In the city, her husband quickly drank himself to death. The woman recalled her years in the city as the best in her life. She worked eight hours a day and then she was free. There was a meal every day at the factory: a first course, a second course, and stewed fruit. Life was good. After work, the whole collective would go stoke the furnaces at a new construction site, voluntarily. They called this the Young Communist Conscription. With pride, she listed the new construction in the city where she had made her contribution. They would stoke the furnaces late into the night, and in the winter they would operate the floodlights. All because they wanted to and enjoyed it. In the evening she'd come home, eat something, and fall into bed. In the morning it was back to the factory. Movies on Sundays. Life had been good.

She'd retired at sixty. Her vision had grown weak, too

weak for a sewing factory. Half a year later, she'd had a stroke. Her neighbors took her to the old folks' home. She'd thought, This is it, the end. Then her ward mate asked her for something to drink. Slowly she got up and helped her neighbor— and drank a little herself, and that seemed to make things easier. She looked around her, in the old folks' home. Everything was fine, she had a roof over her head and food. The only drawback was that it was all fine only as long as her legs held out. If you took to your bed here, no one was going to come to you. They put a plate of hot cereal on your night table—and then you were on your own. Even if you shouted, no one would come. She was scared. Her hands were accustomed to work, they wanted something to do. She started going from room to room spoon-feeding the bedridden. After breakfast she would start her daily rounds. Before she could feed everyone breakfast, it would be time for dinner, and after that supper. Day after day, from breakfast to supper. She never did manage to feed everyone. She decided privately that she would feed only the weakest, those who were at death's door. To those who were a little stronger she would bring bread from dinner and put it into their hands. If you have bread in your hand, you won't die.

It stank in those rooms: the smell of decay and death. The old women often asked for the bedpan, and some asked her to change their sheets. They asked for bedpans more often than food, more often than water. But she wouldn't. She'd decided once and for all that she was only going to feed them.

She would look into a room and ask whether anyone needed feeding. People reacted differently to this harmless question. Some responded proudly, with metal in their voices, that everyone in their room was ambulant; they even screamed and cursed at the feeder. It was an evil omen: The feeder's here—death can't be far behind. This didn't bother her. She just kept going, from room to room.

Worst of all were those who truly did need help. Those who when they had had the strength had shouted at the feeder, driven her away, and reviled her, and who now that they were helpless shouted more loudly than anyone else for help, begging her to feed them, angry when she didn't get there in time for dinner. They gulped down their food, spoon after spoon, keeping an eye on their portion, making sure the feeder didn't snitch any for herself. They lay there like that for a long time, in urine and feces. They rotted away until they had bedsores and ulcers. But they lived. They lived for years. They lived, losing their sanity, not recognizing their benefactor, but persistently opening their mouths for the spoonful of cereal, swallowing greedily, staring into space with their uncomprehending gaze.

It was twilight. We hadn't even noticed half the day passing.

"How many years have you been feeding people, Granny?"

"Thirty-two. Easter it'll be thirty-three. I've got it all counted up. All of it."

"You're a heroine," I said with admiration. "Thirty-two years! Serving people selflessly!"

"Selflessly?"

The feeder shook with delicate, soundless laughter. She quickly crossed herself three times and whispered a prayer.

"You young people really are foolish. You don't understand a thing about life or death."

She looked at me sternly with nasty little eyes. She examined my hands carefully.

"You eat by yourself?"

"Yes."

She sighed. I could tell she was dying to share her secret with someone.

Without looking me in the eye she spat it all out in one breath, precisely and sparingly:

"Selflessly, you say? There were cases when they'd offer me money. Not everyone lying here is an orphan. Their relatives would come and push their filthy lucre into my hands. Only I wouldn't take it. If they slipped it into my pocket I'd give it back to the old folks, down to the last kopek. I bought candies for the ones who couldn't think anymore and fed them every last one. I'm not carrying their money and I don't need their gratitude. I made a pledge. When I came here, at first I fed them out of foolishness, for no real reason. But one day I came to feed one woman and she said to me: Give me the bedpan. I said I wouldn't give bedpans, I'd just feed. Fine, she says, feed me. She filled her mouth with bread, chewed it up, and spit it into my face. All over my face. And now, she said, tie my scarf tighter under my chin so my mouth doesn't fall open when I die. I came to her every day thinking she might change her mind, but she would just give me a stern look and turn away. She lay there for two weeks, dying. That was when I made my pledge that I'd feed everyone if I could. Lots after her refused to eat, and I got used to it. It's just that first one I remember. And I made a pledge to die quietly, not to suffer. I'm weak, I won't have the strength to spit out my bread. But lying there in your own wet is terrible. It gave me a bad scare. And you say 'selflessly.'"

THE PASS

The old folks' home. Not a boarding house or a hospital. A sturdy wall of reinforced concrete slabs and a steel gate. Located in an out-of-the-way part of town. Our neighbors are the lawbreakers in the minimum-security correctional facility next door. It's all out in the open there: prisoners and barbed wire. The prisoners have it good. They serve their sentence and go free. We have nothing to hope for. It's a closed institution. Entry is prohibited to outsiders. The residents don't have the right to leave the institution's gate without written permission from the director. Formal written permission, with signature and stamp. The entrance gate is carefully guarded by a former screw from the neighboring zone. He's too old to work for the prisons and not quite ready to join us. Sit there and open the gate for the bosses. A simple job, familiar, and not a bad bonus to your pension.

If you're healthy and nimble enough you climb the fence or dig your way out. For us, the disabled in wheelchairs, this wretched guard was a real Cerberus.

One young disabled man called a taxi. He got his friends to agree in advance to put him in the car. Three days before his trip he'd obtained a pass. Everything was in order, everything had been planned out: they'd put him in a car here and he'd be met there. He was already in the car and his folding wheelchair was in the trunk.

They drive up to the gate. The driver honks. The short old man with the sharp nasty eyes takes his time coming out of his guard booth.

"Who's in the car?"

The driver doesn't understand the question.

"A person."

"Does he have a pass?"

The nervous driver takes the piece of paper from the invalid and hands it to the watchman. The watchman studies the document closely with a practiced eye.

"All in order, let him pass. I recognize him, he hangs around the gate a lot. Only last time he was in his wheelchair and didn't have a pass."

"But now he does, right? Open the gate."

"You didn't hear me. It's written here, 'pass to leave the territory of the home.' That's the document. I have to follow it precisely. If he wants to walk out, let him; if he doesn't, he doesn't have to. He can't leave the territory of the home in a car."

The driver is irritated. He's not so young anymore and he's not used to losing. He guns the car toward the home and goes inside. After wrangling with the director half an hour he comes out holding the same pass, but with an addition in ink in the margins: "and to ride out." In the corner the institution's seal has been added. The invalid is happy. The director must have been in a good mood that day. According to regulations, the pass should have been canceled and a new application for a pass submitted, and he would have had to wait several days for a decision on this tough question. The car drives up to the gate a second time. The watchman closely examines the amended document, returns it to the taxi driver, and goes reluctantly to open the gate.

They ride in silence for a few minutes. Suddenly the driver stops the car. He grips the steering wheel with both hands and takes a deep breath. Tensely, without looking at his passenger, he speaks almost angrily into the air in front of him.

"Here's the deal, buddy. Don't take this wrong, but I don't want your money. And it's not because you're handicapped. When I was young I did three years and I'll remember it my whole life. I've hated cops ever since."

He flips off his meter and steps on the gas. The car barrels along at top speed away from the old folks' home, the zone, and that bastard of a watchman. This is good. Freedom.

THE FOOL

A bus stop. My wife and I are going somewhere. We're waiting for the bus. The bus finally comes and at the wheel is a young fellow wearing stylish sunglasses. Alla picks me up, puts her right foot on the step, and shifts her weight onto it. All of a sudden the driver smiles in our direction and steps on the gas. The sharp jerk spins Alla around but she jumps to the ground with me in her arms. She lands on her feet; her judo training serves her well. Then she straightens and puts me back in the wheelchair.

A drunken muzhik at the bus stop can't contain his laughter. He laughs long and gaily, and then he approaches us. Alla walks away. She doesn't understand how I can talk to such people.

"He's a fool," he tells me, "a fool, that bus driver."

"Why?"

"Because you have this wheelchair here, and you can see the sun and the birdies on the sidewalk, and what shape he'll be in after some accident nobody knows. His is a dangerous profession."

I get it. I smile. That driver, he really was a fool.

PLAY DOUGH

It's easy to make a papa. Easier than making a mushroom. All you do is roll out two round pieces of play dough.

When I was little, we made things out of play dough. The fat aide gave us each two pieces. One piece we were supposed to roll into a snake; the other into a thin pancake. If you put the snake and the pancake together, you got a mushroom. A simple assignment for kids who weren't so little anymore.

I put my hand on the play dough. I pick up one piece with the other. I try to roll the play dough out on the table. No success. I roll the piece over the table, but it gets thinner, not fatter. I pick up the other one, with the same result.

The other children are coping with their assignment with various results. Some mushrooms are coming out straight and handsome; others, small and lopsided. The aide goes around giving each one of us advice, fixing the caps on some mushrooms and the stems on others. The aide comes over to me.

"What have you come up with?" she asks me gently.

I put one piece on the other. I feel my construction now bears at least some resemblance to a mushroom.

"And what is this? What have you made here?"

The aide takes my play dough and molds it with quick, deft movements of her healthy fingers.

"Now do you see what needs doing?"

I nod. Now I see.

"And now, children, let's see who has the prettiest mushroom. Ruben has the prettiest mushroom."

I stare at the table. The mushroom in front of me really is the straightest and best. I don't care. It isn't my mushroom.

My daughter is making a papa. It's easy to make a papa. Easier than making a mushroom. All you do is roll out two round pieces of play dough. Two identical pieces, the two wheels of a wheelchair.

"And now, children, let's see who has the prettiest mushroom."

NEVER

Never. It's a scary word. The scariest word in the human vo-cabulary. *Never.* The only word comparable to it is *death.* Death is one big never. The eternal never, death sweeps away all hopes and possibilities. No maybes or what ifs. Never.

I'll never climb Everest. I'll never go through long train-ing periods or the necessary medical testing, travel, and ho-tels. I won't curse the weather, the slippery paths, or the steep ledges. There won't be any intermediate stages, mountains big and small—there won't be anything. Maybe, if I'm lucky, if I'm very lucky, I'll see Tibet one day. If I'm incredibly lucky, they'll drop me off from a helicopter at the first staging point, at my first and last impossible. I'll see the mountains, the crazy climbers challenging themselves and nature. After their return—if they're lucky and they do return from the moun-tains without loss of life—they'll tell me joyously and a little abashedly how it all was, there beyond the bounds of my *never.* They'll treat me kindly, I know. I'm just as crazy as they are. It'll be great. Only I'll never climb to the top myself.

I'll never descend in a bathysphere to the Mariana Trench. I won't see how beautiful it is there, at the bottom of the sea. All I can have are videos, documentary confirmation of someone else's persistence and heroism.

They won't take me into outer space either. I'm not wild about barfing from dizziness or floating in a cramped metal box. I'm not wild about it, but it hurts not to be able to. Someone is flying there, overhead, and I can't.

I'll never sail across the English Channel. It won't work to cross the Atlantic on a raft, either. The camels of the Sahara and penguins of Antarctica will have to make do without my attention.

I won't be able to go to sea in a fishing trawler, I won't see a swimming whale, calm and confident in his superiority. They bring me fish straight to my house, bring it in the best possible shape, filleted and ready to cook. Prepackaged—always prepackaged—goods.

I touch the joystick of my electric wheelchair and pull up to the table. I take the plastic straw in my lips and lower it into the glass. Oh, well, if it's prepackaged, then it's prepackaged. Slowly I drink the red wine—prepackaged sun from far-off Argentina. I turn on the television with a click of the remote. I mute it. One channel has a live broadcast of a young people's concert. The little people in the television are happy; they're singing and dancing.

The camera pulls back for a long shot. That guy with the tattoos and earring, I'm sure, is trying to run away from his *never*, too. Not that that makes me feel any better.

BRO

Some friends and I—we are trying to get out to the country. There are no buses and the heat is terrible. There is no point trying to hitchhike. Three healthy guys plus an invalid in a wheelchair—who would pick us up?

Unexpected luck—an army bus. We have no choice; we have to try to get in. The guys lift me and the wheelchair up and try arguing with the driver. The driver keeps saying something about "I'm not supposed to" and "regulations."

From the depths of the bus a soldier hurls himself toward the driver, shouting "Bro-o-o!" He is desperately drunk and in a foul temper. They argue briefly and we're on our way.

The new recruits give us a seat. I'm half-reclining on a low bench, which hurts. My "bro" comes up. He can barely stand, his tunic is unbuttoned, and under it is a striped sailor's jersey.

"Are you from Afghanistan?"

"No."

"Doesn't matter. Before Afghanistan I didn't know what invalids were. Then my friends started coming home without legs and arms, blind. Lots of them couldn't take it and broke. How're you doing?"

"I'm really doing all right. I've got a wife and a job."

"Hang in there. Live."

We get to a town. They lift me out. He shouts something through the glass.

I'll remember you, bro.

I'll remember everything. I'll remember your jersey and your wild eyes.

I'll remember you, bro.

I'll hang in there.

BIG MAC

A white-toothed TV star informs me from the screen in a rapid, energetic voice about the advantages of American democracy. I'm not listening. I know what she's going to say. I'm convinced she's right. She can be proud of her homeland. Its Constitution, anthem, and flag. She has the Bill of Rights, the Statue of Liberty, and McDonald's.

She gives an upbeat spiel about the famous fast-food chain. A sad-eyed clown with an idiotic grin looks at me from a colorful poster. A sandwich and a soda—what could be simpler? A slim American woman in a business suit tries in vain to convince me that this sandwich is the best sandwich, that this soda is the best soda in the world. Nonsense! Food quality is not the most important thing in my life.

I know that all McDonald's restaurants meet world standards for barrier-free access. I know that my wheelchair will move easily through all their doors. The most gracious employees in the world will help me use the toilet, cut my famous Big Mac into small pieces, put a handy straw into a cup with a lid, and lift it to my mouth.

That's it. That's enough. More than enough. For a paralyzed person it's too fabulous a present. A sandwich and a soda. Bread and water. The very basics. Each citizen's guaranteed right to a place in the sun.

Democracy.

"I GO"

The English language. The language of international communication and business negotiations. You can translate almost anything into Russian. From Shakespeare's poetry to a refrigerator manual. Almost anything. Almost.

A wheelchair. An American wheelchair. I have a joystick in my hand. The obedient machine moves my motion-deprived body down the street of a small American town.

I cross the street against the light. This isn't what's so surprising. What's surprising is that I'm crossing a street for the first time in my life. The wheelchair still isn't entirely obedient to the commands of my paralyzed arm.

The cars wait.

A delighted driver sticks his head out of his car, which is in the far left-hand lane. He waves and shouts words of encouragement.

A policeman walks up. He's guessed from my crazed look why I've broken the rules.

"Everything okay?"

"Yes."

"You were absolutely right to go outside. Good luck to you!"

A woman in a wheelchair races by me at full tilt. She has a breathing tube in her mouth. The back of her wheelchair has been lowered to a horizontal position so she can watch the road through a mirror attached to the wheelchair. On the side is a colorful message in big letters: I LOVE LIFE.

A small Chinese restaurant. Narrow doors, four little tables.
The waiter runs out.
"I'm so so sorry. Please accept our official apologies. Unfortunately, your wheelchair won't go through these doors. If it's not too much trouble, you can go into the next room. You won't lose out at all, I assure you. It's the same menu, the same decor, the same chef. We have our certificate, you're welcome to read it. No discrimination here."

I make an embarrassed attempt to calm him down, and assure him that it's no trouble at all for me to go into the next room. He accompanies me to its entrance.

This room is a little bigger. The waiter escorts me to a free table, moving the chairs out of my way.

A few of the restaurant's customers clear their feet from the aisle, but some pay no attention to my chair. When the wheels go over someone's feet, he yelps. No surprise, given the wheelchair's considerable weight. We exchange apologies.

The waiter looks at me in confusion.

"Why do you keep apologizing? You have the same right to eat in this restaurant as they do."

———

A young American in a wheelchair proudly shows me her van with a lift and tells me that all the taxi fleets in America have vans like this.

"Couldn't they have reequipped ordinary pickup trucks for the handicapped? That would have been cheaper," I say.

The girl looks at me in distress and embarrassment.

"But in a refitted truck you could only take one person in a wheelchair. What if it's a boy and a girl? You mean you think they should ride in different cars?"

You can translate almost anything into Russian. From Shakespeare's poetry to a refrigerator manual. Almost everything. Almost.

I could go on and on about America. I could go on and on about the wheelchairs, the "talking" elevators, the smooth roads, the ramps, the vans with lifts. About the blind programmers and the paralyzed scholars. About how I cried when they told me I had to go back to Russia and leave the wheelchair behind. But the feeling I experienced when I put the marvel of American technology in motion for the first time can best be conveyed by the brief yet capacious English sentence "I go." And that's something that doesn't translate into Russian.

HOMELAND

Katya and I stop at a small shop for food. Katya goes to the back of the store while I wait by the entrance. All of the traveler's checks are made out to Katya, since it's hard for me to sign my name. I have a hard time grasping a pen, and my signature doesn't inspire confidence anyway. Katya chooses the food and goes up to the cash register to pay. An elderly Arab is standing behind the counter. He starts arguing heatedly about something with Katya, gesturing desperately. Katya doesn't speak English, so it's up to me to sort this out.

I touch the joystick of my wheelchair and roll up to the counter. Katya steps aside.

"What's the matter?"

"I can't take your check. I don't take checks over ten dollars, and you're giving me one for fifty."

I'm in America. I've been in America for two weeks. I'm calm. I touch the joystick of my wheelchair again. The back of the chair comes up almost to vertical. I ride right up to the counter.

"I see. You mean the check is forged. Look at me. Do you think I'm capable of forging a check? Do I look like an artist? Do I look like a crook? Look at my wheelchair. Do you know how much a wheelchair like this costs? I bought food from you yesterday, I bought from you the day before, I'm buying today, and I hope to buy tomorrow. This is America. You sell and I buy. It's one or the other. If the check is genuine, you sell me your goods. If the check is forged and by me, call the police."

He looks at me respectfully. He obviously likes this approach to the matter.

"Fine. I'll take your check. Are you a Palestinian?"

"No. A Spaniard."

"From Spain?"

"From Russia."

"When are you going home?"

"In three days."

"You must miss your homeland and be looking forward to going home."

"No, I don't miss it."

"Why?"

"It's bad there. There aren't any wheelchairs, or sidewalks, or stores like yours. I don't miss it at all. I'd stay here forever if I could."

He shakes his head reproachfully and looks at me with disdain and a little sadness.

"A boy, you're just a boy. What do you know of life? You can't live here. The people are animals. They'd kill each other for a dollar. I work fourteen hours a day and save my money. I'll save up a little more and go home, to Palestine. But there they shoot guns. They don't shoot guns where you live, right?"

"No."

We pay, say good-bye, and leave. I roll out of the store. I turn the wheelchair around and look through the shop window at the elderly Palestinian. Happy man! He has a homeland.

FREEDOM

San Francisco. The city of my dreams, a place of human habitation in the capitalist hell. A city of odd ducks and outcasts. I'm out on the sidewalk. It's my last day in America. Tomorrow they're taking me to the airport and putting me on a plane. The plane will get me to Russia before my visa runs out. There, in faraway Russia, they'll put me nicely on a couch and sentence me to life imprisonment within four walls. Good Russian people will give me food and drink vodka with me. I'll have plenty to eat and I'll probably be warm. I'll have everything there but freedom. They'll bar me from seeing the sun, roaming through the city, sitting in a café. They'll explain condescendingly that all those are extras, for normal, full-fledged citizens. They'll give me a little more food and vodka and remind me yet again about my black ingratitude. They'll say I want too much, that I need to put up with this a little longer, just a little longer—fifty years or so. I'll agree to everything they say, and nod, detached. I'll obediently do what I'm told and silently endure the disgrace and humiliation. I'll accept my inferiority as an inevitable evil and start breathing more slowly. And when I get sick of this swinish life and ask for a little poison, they'll refuse me, naturally. No speedy deaths in that far-off and humane country. All they'll let me do is poison myself slowly with vodka in hopes of a stomach ulcer or a heart attack.

I'm out on the sidewalk. If I push the throttle as far as it will go, the electric wheelchair's powerful motor will carry me off into the unknown. The plane will fly without me. In a couple of days the wheelchair will run out of charge. I won't survive in this harsh and magnificent country without money or papers. The maximum I can count on is another day of freedom, and then—death.

This is America. Here everything is bought and sold. A terrible, cruel country. You can't count on compassion. But I had my fill of compassion back in Russia. I'm fine with ordinary business.

This is America.

"What's for sale?"

It's my day of freedom. Real freedom. Sun and air. A couple kissing on a park bench. A hippie playing the guitar. The right to see a little girl feeding a squirrel from her hand one more time. The one and only time in my life I'll see a city at night and the blaze of thousands of headlights. Admire for the last time the neon signs, dream of the impossible happiness of being born in this marvelous country. The real deal, the very best quality. Made in America.

"How much does it cost?"

"A little less than life."

"I'll buy it. Keep the change."

After this, in Russia, I drank vodka from dawn to dusk for an entire month, crying through the nights, and in my drunken delirium trying to feel the joystick of my nonexistent, mythical wheelchair. And every day I regretted making the wrong choice at the decisive moment.

NOVOCHERKASSK

I was born in Moscow. Moscow is the capital of Russia. In school we knew everything about Moscow. We sang about Moscow and recited poems. We were told that Moscow was the best, most beautiful city in the world. I don't know. I've only passed through Moscow, and St. Petersburg as well. I'm not about to argue. It may well be that everything they told us was the truth. Maybe that's how it is. Lots of people are sure of that—at least, the Muscovites are.

I've seen three world cities with my own eyes: Novocherkassk, Berkeley, and Madrid. But first there was Novocherkassk.

I'd known about Novocherkassk for a long time. Legends were told about Novocherkassk. People said that at the Novocherkassk children's home they ate potatoes every day, winter and summer. They said tomatoes grew in Novocherkassk. And not just tomatoes. Apricots, watermelons, and cantaloupes grew in that fairy-tale city, walnuts and corn, sweet peppers and squash. I'd tried all these things a couple of times in my life, and I'd read that these fruits and vegetables grew in the south. I'd looked for Novocherkassk on a geographical map of the world, so I knew this city was in the south of Russia. People also said that those who couldn't walk at all were taken away to Novocherkassk, to a home for the elderly and handicapped. A three-story brick building. You could ride around in wheelchairs there, they had attendants and doctors there, people lived for a long time there, and no one died immediately. Of course, all this seemed like a fairy tale, a fiction, an impossible dream. What of it, though? I believed in Novocherkassk. I had to, I had to believe in something.

Sometimes dreams come true. An ordinary lottery ticket turns into a pile of cash, a fern blossoms, and a fairy flies down to see an orphan. One fine, incredible, impossible day, a very important man in Moscow signed a very important piece of paper and they moved me to Novocherkassk. Everything I had so naively believed in turned out to be the truth, even the potatoes and apricots.

I'm young and relatively healthy. I hope to see many more world cities. I'll see Paris and Tokyo, Rome and Sydney, Buenos Aires and Berkeley. I absolutely must see Berkeley again. I believe that all these cities do in fact exist in the world. I believe it the way I once believed in Novocherkassk.

I was born in Moscow. I was very, very unlucky to be born in that terrible, insane city. I was lucky in Novocherkassk. Novocherkassk is a fine city. I would have died if there hadn't been a Novocherkassk in Russia.

BLACK

As always in life, black and white alternate, and disappointment follows success. Everything changes. Everything has to change. That's the way it's supposed to be, that's how things work. I know this, I'm not against it, I can only hope. Hope for a miracle. I sincerely wish, I passionately want my black period to last a little longer and not switch to white.

I don't like white. White is the color of impotence and doom, the color of hospital ceilings and white sheets. Guaranteed care, silence, and calm: nothing. The permanent nothing of hospital life.

Black is the color of struggle and hope. The color of the night sky, the confident and precise backdrop of dreams, the temporary lulls between the white, the endless daytime periods of my bodily infirmities. The color of dreams and fairy tales, the color of the inner world behind my closed eyes. The color of freedom, the color I chose for my electric wheelchair.

And when my turn comes to go down the line of impersonal, well-meaning mannequins in white lab coats and I reach my end, my very own eternal night, I'll leave only letters behind. My letters. My black letters on a white background. I hope.

acknowledgments

Thanks to Eve, our Foremother, for eating the apple.
Thanks to Adam, for taking part.
Special thanks to Eve.

Thanks to my grandmother Esperanza for bearing my mama.
Thanks to Ignacio for taking part.
Special thanks to my grandmother.

Thanks to my mama for bearing me.
Thanks to David for taking part.
Special thanks to my mama.

Thanks to my mama for bearing my sister.
Thanks to Sergei for taking part.
Special thanks to my mama.

Thanks to my literature teacher. Once when I was sick, she brought me chicken soup. She brought jam to class, and we ate jam and were perfectly happy. When I wrote compositions, she gave me the highest mark, when she didn't give me the lowest.